The French Laundry Feast: 95 Culinary Inspirations from Thomas Keller's Masterful Menu

Hoisup Taro Leaves Corned

Copyright © 2023 Hoisup Taro Leaves Corned
All rights reserved.
:

Contents

INTRODUCTION ... 8
1. Gougères ... 10
2. Oysters and Pearls ... 11
3. Salmon Tartare Cornet ... 13
4. Caviar and Crème Fraîche ... 14
5. Oyster and Absinthe ... 16
6. Garden Carrot "Tabbouleh" ... 18
7. Grilled Hawaiian Hearts of Peach Palm ... 19
8. Hen Egg Custard ... 21
9. Black Truffle Custard ... 23
10. Butter-Poached Maine Lobster ... 24
11. White Truffle Oil-Infused Custard ... 26
12. Beet "Tartare" ... 27
13. Cauliflower "Panna Cotta" ... 29
14. Sweet Butter-Poached Maine Lobster ... 31
15. Yukon Gold Potato "Levée" ... 32
16. "Salad" of Hawaiian Hearts of Peach Palm ... 34
17. Sauteed Fillet of Gulf Coast Cobia ... 36
18. Slowly Poached Moulard Duck Foie Gras ... 37
19. Carnaroli Risotto Biologico ... 39
20. Chatham Bay Cod "Brandade" ... 41
21. Nantes Carrot "Vichyssoise" ... 42
22. Freshwater Eel "Savarin" ... 44
23. Herb-Crusted Sautéed Fillet of Pacific Sturgeon ... 46
24. Sweet Butter-Poached Maine Lobster Tail ... 47
25. "Tongue in Cheek" Creekstone Farm Beef Cheeks ... 49
26. "Chaud-Froid" of Poularde ... 50
27. Slow-Roasted Liberty Duck Breast ... 52

28. Alaskan King Crab "Cassoulet" 54

29. Herb-Grilled Saddle of Elysian Fields Farm Lamb 56

30. Roasted Elysian Fields Farm Baby Lamb 58

31. Pave of Kindai Maguro Tuna 59

32. Sauteed Fillet of John Dory 61

33. Brandt Beef Short Rib "Bourguignon" 62

34. Lobster "Bouillabaisse" 64

35. Red Wine-Braised Beef Cheeks 66

36. "Pastrami" of Liberty Farm Duck 68

37. Snake River Farms Pork Jowl 70

38. Pan-Roasted Breast of Four Story Hill Farm's Poularde 71

39. "Galette de Pommes de Terre" 73

40. Sweet Butter-Poached Maine Lobster Medallions 75

41. "Poulet Rôti" 76

42. Marcho Farms Veal Sweetbreads 78

43. Sweet Butter-Poached Maine Lobster Knuckle Sandwich 80

44. Roasted Rack of Elysian Fields Farm Lamb 81

45. "Ballotine" of Liberty Farms Pekin Duck Foie Gras 83

46. Broiled Japanese Bluefin Tuna 85

47. Sauteed Fillet of Mediterranean Loup de Mer 86

48. Snake River Farms Pork Belly Confit 88

49. Roasted Sirloin of Brandt Beef 90

50. Crispy-Skinned Striped Bass 92

51. "Oeufs et Oignons" 93

52. Pan-Seared Fillet of Gulf Coast Cobia 95

53. Herb-Crusted Sautéed Fillet of Alaskan King Salmon 97

54. Pan-Roasted Maine Lobster Tail 98

55. Seared Brandt Beef Tenderloin 100

56. Grilled Japanese Wagyu Ribeye 101

57. Roasted Venison Loin 103

58. "Boudin Noir" 105

59. Crispy Skin Suckling Pig 106

60. Roasted Saddle of Elysian Fields Farm Lamb 108

61. "Gâteau Basque" 110

62. "Rouelle" 112

63. Coconut Sorbet 113

64. "Palet d'Or" 115

65. "Café Liégeois" 116

66. "Nougatine" 118

67. "Profiteroles" 120

68. "Kaffir Lime" 122

69. "Baba au Rhum" 123

70. "Religieuse" 125

71. "Pavlova" 127

72. "Savarin au Mille-Feuille" 129

73. "Mille-Feuille" 131

74. "Meringue" 133

75. "Macaron" 134

76. "Canele" 136

77. "Tarte au Citron" 138

78. "Charlotte Russe" 140

79. "Pots de Crème" 142

80. "Tarte Tatin" 144

81. "Pain Perdu" 145

82. "Soufflé" 147

83. "Brioche" 149

84. "Praline" 151

85. "Madeleine" 152

86. "Coulis" 154
87. "Pâte à Choux" 156
88. "Crêpe" 157
89. "Fondant" 159
90. "Crème Brûlée" 160
91. "Éclair" 162
92. "Parfait" 164
93. "Gâteau" 166
94. "Sorbet" 168
95. "Panna Cotta" 170
CONCLUSION 172

INTRODUCTION

Embark on a gastronomic journey through the hallowed halls of culinary brilliance with "The French Laundry Feast: 95 Culinary Inspirations from Thomas Keller's Masterful Menu." This cookbook is a celebration of the iconic and transformative dining experience offered by Thomas Keller's legendary restaurant, The French Laundry. Nestled in the quaint town of Yountville, California, The French Laundry has earned its place as a culinary mecca, drawing food enthusiasts and connoisseurs from around the globe.

Thomas Keller, a virtuoso in the world of haute cuisine, has redefined the art of fine dining with his meticulous attention to detail, unwavering commitment to excellence, and a profound respect for the craft. The French Laundry Feast pays homage to Keller's culinary genius, presenting 95 meticulously crafted recipes inspired by the masterful menu that has left an indelible mark on the palates of those fortunate enough to experience it.

At the heart of this cookbook lies a dedication to capturing the essence of The French Laundry's culinary magic. Each recipe serves as a portal into the world of refined flavors, innovative techniques, and the profound artistry that defines Keller's culinary philosophy. Whether you're a seasoned home cook or an aspiring chef, this collection provides a rare opportunity to recreate the essence of The French Laundry in the comfort of your own kitchen.

The journey begins with a deep dive into the history and ethos of The French Laundry, exploring its inception, evolution, and the principles that have guided Keller's culinary vision. From the meticulous sourcing of ingredients to the precision of execution, every aspect of The French Laundry's culinary approach is dissected, offering readers a behind-the-scenes glimpse into the inner workings of this culinary institution.

The 95 culinary inspirations presented in this cookbook reflect the diverse and exquisite offerings found on The French Laundry's menu. From the iconic Oysters and Pearls to the sublime Butter-Poached Lobster and the ethereal Coffee and Doughnuts dessert, each recipe is a testament to the artistry and innovation that define Keller's signature style. The cookbook is thoughtfully organized, allowing readers to explore appetizers, main courses, desserts, and everything in between, mirroring the progression of a meal at The French Laundry.

Accompanying the recipes are vibrant anecdotes and insights that provide context to the dishes, offering a deeper understanding of the inspiration behind each creation. The French Laundry Feast is not merely a collection of recipes; it is a culinary odyssey that invites readers to immerse themselves in the spirit of Thomas Keller's culinary excellence.

Whether you are looking to recreate a cherished dining experience, elevate your culinary skills, or simply savor the flavors of a world-renowned restaurant, "The French Laundry Feast" is your passport to the extraordinary. Join us on this culinary adventure as we pay homage to Thomas Keller's enduring legacy and invite you to bring the magic of The French Laundry into your own kitchen.

1. Gougères

Gougères are delightful French cheese puffs, often served as appetizers or snacks. Originating from Burgundy, these airy, savory pastries are made with choux pastry dough and grated Gruyère cheese, resulting in a perfect blend of crispiness and cheesy goodness. They pair beautifully with a glass of wine or can be enjoyed on their own as a delectable treat.

Serving: This recipe makes approximately 24 gougères. Serve them warm as an appetizer alongside a glass of Champagne or a light white wine for an elegant touch.
Preparation time: 15 minutes
Ready time: 40 minutes
Cooking time: 25 minutes

Ingredients:
- 1 cup water
- 6 tablespoons unsalted butter
- 1/2 teaspoon salt
- 1 cup all-purpose flour
- 4 large eggs
- 1 1/2 cups grated Gruyère cheese (or other flavorful cheese like Comté)
- Pinch of nutmeg (optional)
- Pinch of black pepper (optional)

Instructions:
1. Preheat your oven to 425°F (220°C). Line a baking sheet with parchment paper or lightly grease it.
2. In a saucepan over medium heat, combine the water, butter, and salt. Bring the mixture to a boil, stirring occasionally.
3. Once the mixture is boiling, reduce the heat to low and add the flour all at once. Stir vigorously with a wooden spoon until the mixture forms a ball and pulls away from the sides of the pan, about 2-3 minutes.
4. Transfer the dough to a mixing bowl and let it cool for a few minutes. Then, using a hand mixer or stand mixer, beat in the eggs one at a time, ensuring each egg is fully incorporated before adding the next. The dough should be smooth and glossy.

5. Stir in the grated cheese, nutmeg (if using), and black pepper (if using) until well combined.
6. Using a spoon or a piping bag, drop tablespoon-sized mounds of dough onto the prepared baking sheet, leaving space between them for expansion.
7. Bake in the preheated oven for 10 minutes, then reduce the heat to 375°F (190°C) and continue baking for an additional 15-20 minutes or until the gougères are golden brown and puffed.
8. Once done, remove from the oven and let the gougères cool slightly before serving. They are best enjoyed warm.

Nutrition Information (per gougère, approximate):
- Calories: 90
- Total Fat: 7g
- Saturated Fat: 4g
- Cholesterol: 55mg
- Sodium: 110mg
- Total Carbohydrate: 3g
- Protein: 4g

Note: Nutritional values are approximate and may vary based on specific ingredients used.

2. Oysters and Pearls

'Oysters and Pearls" is a celebrated dish from Thomas Keller's renowned The French Laundry restaurant, renowned for its exquisite blend of flavors and luxurious ingredients. This dish showcases the delicate harmony between fresh oysters, tapioca pearls, and a creamy sabayon sauce. Elegant and sophisticated, it's a culinary masterpiece that embodies the essence of fine dining.

Serving: 4 servings
Preparation time: 30 minutes
Ready time: 1 hour

Ingredients:
- 24 fresh oysters, shucked
- 1 cup pearl tapioca

- 4 cups chicken stock
- 2 cups heavy cream
- 4 egg yolks
- Salt to taste
- White pepper to taste
- 1 tablespoon chives, finely chopped (for garnish)
- 1 tablespoon caviar (optional, for garnish)

Instructions:
1. Prepare the Tapioca Pearls:
- Rinse the pearl tapioca under cold water and drain.
- In a saucepan, bring the chicken stock to a boil.
- Add the tapioca pearls to the boiling stock, reduce the heat to a simmer, and cook for about 20-25 minutes or until the pearls are translucent and tender. Stir occasionally to prevent sticking.
- Once cooked, strain the tapioca pearls and set them aside.
2. Prepare the Sabayon Sauce:
- In a separate saucepan, heat the heavy cream over medium heat until it begins to simmer. Reduce the heat to low.
- In a heatproof bowl, whisk the egg yolks until slightly thickened.
- Slowly pour the warm heavy cream into the egg yolks while continuously whisking to temper the eggs.
- Return the mixture to the saucepan and cook over low heat, stirring constantly, until the sauce coats the back of a spoon. Be careful not to let it boil.
- Season the sabayon with salt and white pepper to taste. Remove from heat and set aside.
3. Assemble the Dish:
- Preheat the broiler.
- Place the shucked oysters on a baking dish and broil for 2-3 minutes, just until they begin to curl at the edges.
- In individual serving dishes or shallow bowls, spoon a layer of the cooked tapioca pearls.
- Top the pearls with 3 broiled oysters per serving.
- Carefully spoon the warm sabayon sauce over the oysters, ensuring it covers them evenly.
- Garnish with finely chopped chives and a dollop of caviar, if desired.
4. Serve: Serve immediately to enjoy the dish at its best.

Nutrition Information *(per serving, without optional caviar)*:

- Calories: Approximately 380
- Fat: 28g
- Saturated Fat: 16g
- Cholesterol: 285mg
- Sodium: 620mg
- Carbohydrates: 17g
- Fiber: 0.5g
- Sugars: 2g
- Protein: 14g

Note: Nutritional values are approximate and can vary based on specific ingredients used.

3. Salmon Tartare Cornet

Indulge in the exquisite flavors inspired by the iconic dishes of Thomas Keller's The French Laundry with this sophisticated Salmon Tartare Cornet. A play on textures and tastes, this dish encapsulates the freshness of salmon complemented by vibrant herbs and zesty accents, all enclosed in a delicate cornet. Perfect for elevating any dining experience.

Serving: Serves: 4
Serving Size: 1 cornet
Preparation time: 20 minutes
Ready time: 30 minutes

Ingredients:
- 8 ounces fresh sushi-grade salmon, finely diced
- 2 tablespoons finely chopped shallots
- 1 tablespoon capers, drained and chopped
- 1 tablespoon fresh chives, finely chopped
- 1 tablespoon fresh dill, finely chopped
- Zest of 1 lemon
- 1 teaspoon Dijon mustard
- 1 tablespoon extra-virgin olive oil
- Salt and freshly ground black pepper, to taste
- 4-6 store-bought large cornets or tuile cones
- Microgreens or small herb sprigs for garnish (optional)

Instructions:
1. In a mixing bowl, combine the diced salmon, shallots, capers, chives, dill, lemon zest, Dijon mustard, and olive oil.
2. Gently fold the ingredients together until well incorporated. Season with salt and freshly ground black pepper to taste.
3. Cover the salmon mixture and refrigerate for at least 10-15 minutes to allow the flavors to meld together.
4. Meanwhile, prepare the cornets or tuile cones according to the package instructions if they need any assembling or baking.
5. Once the salmon mixture has marinated, carefully spoon it into the prepared cornets or tuile cones.
6. Garnish each cornet with microgreens or small herb sprigs, if desired.
7. Serve immediately to enjoy the freshness of the salmon tartare within the delicate cornet.

Nutrition Information (per serving):
- Calories: 180
- Total Fat: 10g
- Saturated Fat: 1.5g
- Cholesterol: 40mg
- Sodium: 280mg
- Total Carbohydrates: 6g
- Dietary Fiber: 0.5g
- Sugars: 1g
- Protein: 17g

Note: Nutrition Information is approximate and may vary based on specific ingredients used.

Enjoy the delightful blend of flavors and textures in this elegant Salmon Tartare Cornet, an ode to the culinary brilliance of The French Laundry!

4. Caviar and Crème Fraîche

Elevate your culinary experience with this exquisite dish inspired by the legendary Thomas Keller's The French Laundry restaurant. Caviar and Crème Fraîche, a timeless pairing that embodies sophistication and indulgence. The delicate pearls of caviar harmonize with the luxurious richness of crème fraîche, creating a symphony of flavors that is sure to captivate your taste buds. This recipe celebrates the essence of fine dining, inviting you to savor a moment of culinary perfection.

Serving: Ideal for special occasions, this recipe serves 4 as an elegant appetizer or canape.
Preparation Time: 15 minutes
Ready Time: 15 minutes

Ingredients:
- 1 ounce (30g) high-quality caviar (such as Osetra or Beluga)
- 1 cup (240g) crème fraîche
- 1 tablespoon chopped fresh chives
- 1 lemon, cut into wedges
- Freshly ground black pepper
- 16 small, thin slices of brioche or melba toast

Instructions:
1. Prepare the Crème Fraîche Mixture:
- In a bowl, gently fold the chopped chives into the crème fraîche until well combined. Refrigerate until ready to use.
2. Assemble the Dish:
- Arrange the brioche or melba toast slices on a serving platter.
- Spoon a small dollop of the chive-infused crème fraîche onto each slice.
3. Top with Caviar:
- Using a non-metallic spoon, carefully place a small amount of caviar on top of the crème fraîche on each toast.
4. Garnish:
- Sprinkle a pinch of freshly ground black pepper over the caviar.
5. Serve:
- Garnish the platter with lemon wedges and serve immediately.

Nutrition Information:
(Per Serving)
- Calories: 220
- Total Fat: 18g
- Saturated Fat: 10g
- Trans Fat: 0g
- Cholesterol: 70mg
- Sodium: 180mg
- Total Carbohydrates: 5g

- Dietary Fiber: 0g
- Sugars: 1g
- Protein: 8g

Indulge in the luxurious simplicity of Caviar and Crème Fraîche, a dish that pays homage to the culinary finesse of The French Laundry. Delight your guests with this elegant appetizer, where each bite is a celebration of flavor and refinement.

5. Oyster and Absinthe

Indulge in the exquisite marriage of flavors with our "Oyster and Absinthe" dish, inspired by the culinary finesse of Thomas Keller's iconic restaurant, The French Laundry. This recipe captures the essence of fine dining, bringing together the briny richness of oysters and the subtle herbal notes of absinthe. Elevate your dining experience with this sophisticated dish that pays homage to the culinary mastery of one of the world's renowned chefs.

Serving: 4 servings
Preparation Time: 20 minutes
Ready Time: 30 minutes

Ingredients:
- 24 fresh oysters, shucked
- 1/4 cup absinthe
- 1/2 cup heavy cream
- 2 tablespoons unsalted butter
- 2 shallots, finely chopped
- 2 cloves garlic, minced
- Salt and black pepper to taste
- Fresh chives, finely chopped (for garnish)
- Crushed ice (for serving)

Instructions:
1. Prepare the Oysters:
- Shuck the fresh oysters, discarding any shell fragments. Place them on a bed of crushed ice to keep them chilled.
2. Absinthe Reduction:

- In a small saucepan, heat absinthe over low heat until it simmers. Allow it to reduce by half, then set aside.

3. Creamy Shallot-Garlic Sauce:
- In a separate saucepan, melt butter over medium heat. Add chopped shallots and minced garlic, sautéing until softened.
- Pour in the heavy cream, stirring continuously. Allow the mixture to simmer until it thickens.
- Season with salt and black pepper to taste.

4. Combine Flavors:
- Gently pour the reduced absinthe into the creamy shallot-garlic sauce, stirring to combine. Simmer for an additional 2-3 minutes to let the flavors meld.

5. Cook the Oysters:
- Place each shucked oyster in a heatproof serving dish or shell. Spoon a small amount of the absinthe-cream sauce over each oyster.

6. Broil or Bake:
- Preheat your broiler or oven. Place the oysters under the broiler or in the oven until the sauce is bubbly and lightly browned, approximately 5 minutes.

7. Garnish and Serve:
- Remove the oysters from heat and sprinkle with fresh chives. Serve immediately on a bed of crushed ice for a delightful contrast in temperatures.

Nutrition Information:
(Per serving)
- Calories: 220
- Fat: 16g
- Saturated Fat: 10g
- Cholesterol: 90mg
- Sodium: 180mg
- Carbohydrates: 6g
- Fiber: 0.5g
- Sugar: 1g
- Protein: 12g

Elevate your culinary repertoire with this sophisticated Oyster and Absinthe dish, embodying the culinary excellence inspired by Thomas Keller's The French Laundry.

6. Garden Carrot "Tabbouleh"

Indulge in the vibrant flavors of Thomas Keller's culinary mastery with our Garden Carrot Tabbouleh—an innovative twist on the classic Tabbouleh that combines the freshness of garden-fresh carrots with the finesse of The French Laundry. This dish is a celebration of colors, textures, and tastes, showcasing the commitment to quality ingredients that defines Keller's renowned cuisine.

Serving: 4 servings
Preparation Time: 15 minutes
Ready Time: 30 minutes

Ingredients:
- 1 cup bulgur wheat
- 2 cups boiling water
- 1 bunch fresh garden carrots, grated
- 1 cup cherry tomatoes, halved
- 1 cucumber, diced
- 1/2 cup red onion, finely chopped
- 1/2 cup fresh parsley, chopped
- 1/4 cup fresh mint, chopped
- Zest and juice of 2 lemons
- 1/4 cup extra-virgin olive oil
- Salt and pepper to taste

Instructions:
1. Place the bulgur wheat in a large bowl and pour the boiling water over it. Cover the bowl with a lid or plastic wrap and let it sit for 15-20 minutes until the bulgur is tender and has absorbed the water.
2. In the meantime, prepare the vegetables. Grate the garden-fresh carrots, halve the cherry tomatoes, dice the cucumber, finely chop the red onion, and chop the fresh parsley and mint.
3. Once the bulgur is ready, fluff it with a fork to separate the grains. Allow it to cool to room temperature.
4. In a large mixing bowl, combine the cooled bulgur with the grated carrots, cherry tomatoes, cucumber, red onion, parsley, and mint.
5. In a separate small bowl, whisk together the lemon zest, lemon juice, and extra-virgin olive oil. Season with salt and pepper to taste.

6. Pour the dressing over the tabbouleh mixture and toss everything together until well combined.
7. Allow the flavors to meld by refrigerating the tabbouleh for at least 10 minutes before serving.
8. Serve chilled and garnish with additional fresh mint or parsley if desired.

Nutrition Information:
Note: Nutrition information is approximate and may vary based on specific ingredients used.
- Calories per serving: 250
- Total Fat: 10g
- Saturated Fat: 1.5g
- Cholesterol: 0mg
- Sodium: 150mg
- Total Carbohydrates: 35g
- Dietary Fiber: 8g
- Sugars: 5g
- Protein: 6g

Elevate your dining experience with this Garden Carrot Tabbouleh, a delightful tribute to the culinary excellence that defines Thomas Keller's iconic restaurant, The French Laundry.

7. Grilled Hawaiian Hearts of Peach Palm

Inspired by the culinary excellence of Thomas Keller's The French Laundry, this recipe for Grilled Hawaiian Hearts of Peach Palm is a delightful homage to the restaurant's commitment to exquisite flavors and fine dining. The dish combines the tropical essence of Hawaiian ingredients with a touch of sophistication, inviting you to savor the symphony of flavors in every bite.

Serving: 4 servings
Preparation Time: 15 minutes
Ready Time: 30 minutes

Ingredients:
- 2 cans (14 ounces each) hearts of peach palm, drained

- 1/4 cup olive oil
- 2 tablespoons honey
- 2 tablespoons soy sauce
- 1 tablespoon rice vinegar
- 1 teaspoon grated fresh ginger
- 2 cloves garlic, minced
- Salt and black pepper to taste
- Fresh cilantro, chopped (for garnish)
- Pineapple salsa (optional, for serving)

Instructions:
1. Preheat the Grill:
- Preheat your grill to medium-high heat.
2. Prepare the Marinade:
- In a small bowl, whisk together the olive oil, honey, soy sauce, rice vinegar, grated ginger, minced garlic, salt, and black pepper. This flavorful marinade will infuse the hearts of peach palm with a perfect balance of sweet and savory notes.
3. Marinate the Peach Palm:
- Place the drained hearts of peach palm in a shallow dish. Pour the marinade over the peach palm, ensuring each piece is well coated. Allow them to marinate for at least 10 minutes, allowing the flavors to penetrate.
4. Grill the Peach Palm:
- Place the marinated hearts of peach palm on the preheated grill. Grill for 5-7 minutes, turning occasionally, until they develop grill marks and a delightful char.
5. Garnish and Serve:
- Remove the grilled peach palm from the grill and transfer them to a serving platter. Garnish with fresh chopped cilantro and serve with pineapple salsa on the side for an extra burst of tropical flavor.
6. Enjoy:
- Relish in the unique blend of flavors and textures in every bite of these Grilled Hawaiian Hearts of Peach Palm, inspired by the culinary excellence of Thomas Keller's The French Laundry.

Nutrition Information:
- *Note: Nutrition information is approximate and may vary based on specific ingredients used.*
- Calories per serving: 200

- Total Fat: 12g
- Cholesterol: 0mg
- Sodium: 400mg
- Total Carbohydrates: 22g
- Dietary Fiber: 3g
- Sugars: 10g
- Protein: 2g

Indulge in the sophistication of this dish, embracing the tropical charm of Hawaiian cuisine elevated by the culinary inspiration from The French Laundry.

8. Hen Egg Custard

Indulge your palate in the exquisite world of French culinary excellence with this luxurious Hen Egg Custard recipe inspired by the renowned menu of Thomas Keller's The French Laundry restaurant. Elevate your dining experience with the velvety smoothness of custard, crafted to perfection with the finest hen eggs and a touch of culinary finesse.

Serving: 4 servings
Preparation Time: 15 minutes
Ready Time: 1 hour 30 minutes

Ingredients:
- 6 fresh hen eggs
- 2 cups heavy cream
- 1 cup whole milk
- 1/2 teaspoon salt
- 1/4 teaspoon white pepper
- Pinch of freshly grated nutmeg
- 1 teaspoon truffle oil (optional, for a decadent twist)
- Fresh chives, finely chopped, for garnish

Instructions:
1. Preheat the Oven:
Preheat your oven to 325°F (163°C). Place four ramekins in a baking dish and set aside.
2. Prepare the Custard Mixture:

In a mixing bowl, whisk together the hen eggs, heavy cream, whole milk, salt, white pepper, and a pinch of freshly grated nutmeg until well combined. For an extra layer of indulgence, consider adding a teaspoon of truffle oil to elevate the flavor profile.

3. Strain the Mixture:

Strain the custard mixture through a fine-mesh sieve into another bowl. This step ensures a silky-smooth texture, free from any lumps.

4. Divide into Ramekins:

Pour the custard mixture evenly into the prepared ramekins in the baking dish.

5. Create a Water Bath:

Carefully pour hot water into the baking dish, creating a water bath around the ramekins. The water should reach halfway up the sides of the ramekins.

6. Bake to Perfection:

Place the baking dish in the preheated oven and bake for approximately 45-50 minutes or until the custard is set around the edges but still slightly jiggly in the center.

7. Chill and Garnish:

Remove the ramekins from the water bath and allow the custard to cool to room temperature. Refrigerate for at least 1 hour before serving. Just before serving, sprinkle finely chopped fresh chives for a burst of color and added freshness.

Nutrition Information:

(Per serving)
- Calories: 380
- Total Fat: 32g
- Saturated Fat: 18g
- Cholesterol: 310mg
- Sodium: 380mg
- Total Carbohydrates: 6g
- Sugars: 4g
- Protein: 12g

Indulge in the divine richness of this Hen Egg Custard, a culinary masterpiece that mirrors the sophistication of Thomas Keller's The French Laundry. Perfect for an elegant dinner party or a special treat, this custard will leave an indelible mark on your taste buds.

9. Black Truffle Custard

Indulge your palate in the exquisite world of culinary sophistication with this decadent Black Truffle Custard, inspired by the renowned menu of Thomas Keller's iconic restaurant, The French Laundry. Elevating the ordinary into the extraordinary, this dish marries the richness of custard with the earthy and aromatic essence of black truffles, creating a symphony of flavors that dance on your taste buds. Perfect for those special occasions when you want to savor the finer things in life.

Serving: Serves 4
Preparation Time: 20 minutes
Ready Time: 1 hour and 30 minutes

Ingredients:
- 4 large eggs
- 2 cups heavy cream
- 1/4 teaspoon white pepper
- 1/4 teaspoon kosher salt
- 1/2 teaspoon truffle oil
- 1 tablespoon black truffle, finely chopped
- 1 teaspoon chives, finely chopped (for garnish)

Instructions:
1. Preheat the Oven:
Preheat your oven to 325°F (163°C). Place four ramekins in a deep baking dish.
2. Whisk the Eggs:
In a mixing bowl, whisk the eggs until they are well beaten.
3. Prepare the Custard Base:
In a saucepan over medium heat, combine the heavy cream, white pepper, and kosher salt. Heat the mixture until it is just about to simmer, then remove it from the heat.
4. Temper the Eggs:
Slowly pour a small amount of the hot cream mixture into the beaten eggs, whisking constantly to avoid curdling. Gradually incorporate the remaining cream into the eggs.
5. Add Truffle Flavor:
Stir in the truffle oil and finely chopped black truffle, ensuring an even distribution of the truffle flavor throughout the custard.

6. Strain the Mixture:
Strain the custard mixture through a fine-mesh sieve into a bowl to achieve a smooth and velvety texture.
7. Fill the Ramekins:
Pour the custard mixture evenly into the prepared ramekins.
8. Bake in a Water Bath:
Place the baking dish with the ramekins in the preheated oven. Fill the baking dish with hot water until it reaches halfway up the sides of the ramekins. This water bath ensures a gentle and even cooking process.
9. Bake Until Set:
Bake for approximately 45-50 minutes or until the custard is set but still slightly jiggly in the center.
10. Chill and Garnish:
Remove the ramekins from the water bath and let them cool to room temperature. Refrigerate for at least 1 hour. Before serving, sprinkle chopped chives on top for a burst of freshness.

Nutrition Information:
Per Serving
- Calories: 420
- Total Fat: 38g
- Saturated Fat: 22g
- Trans Fat: 0g
- Cholesterol: 310mg
- Sodium: 220mg
- Total Carbohydrates: 3g
- Dietary Fiber: 0g
- Sugars: 1g
- Protein: 10g

Delight your senses with the luxurious Black Truffle Custard—a testament to the refined and innovative cuisine that defines Thomas Keller's culinary legacy at The French Laundry.

10. Butter-Poached Maine Lobster

Indulge in the luxurious flavors of the iconic French Laundry with this exquisite Butter-Poached Maine Lobster recipe. Drawing inspiration from Thomas Keller's renowned culinary expertise, this dish encapsulates the essence of fine dining and brings the essence of the sea to your plate.

Serving: 2 servings
Preparation time: 20 minutes
Ready time: 40 minutes

Ingredients:
- 2 live Maine lobsters (about 1 1/2 pounds each)
- 1 cup unsalted butter, cubed
- 2 cloves garlic, crushed
- 2 sprigs fresh thyme
- Salt and freshly ground black pepper to taste
- 1 lemon, cut into wedges for garnish
- Chives or parsley for garnish (optional)

Instructions:
1. Prepare the lobsters by bringing a large pot of water to a boil. Add a generous amount of salt to the water.
2. Carefully add the live lobsters to the boiling water and cook for about 3-4 minutes until they turn bright red.
3. Remove the lobsters from the boiling water and immediately place them in an ice bath to stop the cooking process.
4. Once cooled, remove the lobster meat from the shells. Cut the meat into bite-sized pieces and set aside.
5. In a large saucepan over low heat, melt the butter until it begins to foam. Add the crushed garlic and thyme sprigs, allowing the flavors to infuse into the butter for about 5 minutes.
6. Increase the heat to a gentle simmer. Add the lobster pieces to the saucepan, ensuring they are fully submerged in the butter.
7. Poach the lobster in the butter for 8-10 minutes, maintaining a low simmer, until the lobster is just cooked through and tender.
8. Season with salt and freshly ground black pepper to taste.
9. Using a slotted spoon, carefully remove the lobster pieces from the butter and transfer them to serving plates.
10. Strain the butter sauce through a fine-mesh sieve, discarding the garlic and thyme.
11. Drizzle the strained butter sauce over the plated lobster pieces. Garnish with lemon wedges and chopped chives or parsley if desired.

12. Serve immediately and savor the decadent flavors of this buttery delight.

Nutrition Information: (Approximate values per serving)
- Calories: 550 kcal
- Protein: 28g
- Fat: 45g
- Carbohydrates: 2g
- Fiber: 0.5g
- Sugar: 0.5g
- Sodium: 920mg

Note: Nutritional values may vary depending on the size of lobsters and exact quantities of ingredients used.

11. White Truffle Oil-Infused Custard

Indulge in the luxurious flavors of The French Laundry with this exquisite White Truffle Oil-Infused Custard recipe. Inspired by the refined menu of Thomas Keller's esteemed restaurant, this dish encapsulates elegance and depth, marrying the delicate custard with the aromatic essence of white truffle oil.

Serving: This recipe yields 4 servings, perfect for an intimate gathering or a decadent personal treat.
Preparation Time: Preparation takes approximately 15 minutes.
Ready Time: Allow 1 hour and 30 minutes for cooking and cooling.

Ingredients:
- 2 cups heavy cream
- 4 large egg yolks
- 1/4 cup granulated sugar
- 1 teaspoon white truffle oil
- Pinch of salt
- Fresh chives, finely chopped (for garnish)

Instructions:
1. Preheat your oven to 300°F (150°C). Arrange four ramekins in a deep baking dish.

2. In a saucepan over medium heat, pour the heavy cream and bring it to a gentle simmer. Stir occasionally to prevent scalding.
3. In a mixing bowl, whisk together the egg yolks, sugar, white truffle oil, and a pinch of salt until well combined and slightly thickened.
4. Gradually pour the hot cream into the egg mixture, whisking continuously to temper the eggs.
5. Strain the custard mixture through a fine-mesh sieve into a pouring jug or bowl to ensure a smooth consistency.
6. Divide the custard evenly among the prepared ramekins. Carefully pour hot water into the baking dish, filling it halfway up the sides of the ramekins.
7. Gently transfer the baking dish to the oven and bake the custards for 40-45 minutes, or until the edges are set but the center still jiggles slightly when tapped.
8. Remove the baking dish from the oven and let the custards cool in the water bath for 20-30 minutes.
9. Carefully remove the ramekins from the water bath, cover them with plastic wrap, and refrigerate for at least 1 hour to chill and set.
10. Before serving, garnish each custard with a sprinkle of finely chopped fresh chives for an added layer of flavor and freshness.

Nutrition Information (per serving):
Calories: 420
Total Fat: 38g
Saturated Fat: 22g
Cholesterol: 300mg
Sodium: 50mg
Total Carbohydrate: 16g
Sugars: 14g
Protein: 5g
Enjoy the harmonious blend of creamy custard and the distinct aroma of white truffle oil, a delightful homage to the refined cuisine of The French Laundry.

12. Beet "Tartare"

Beet "Tartare" is a vibrant, plant-based twist on the classic beef tartare, inspired by the innovative menu of Thomas Keller's renowned The

French Laundry restaurant. This dish celebrates the earthy sweetness of beets, finely diced and seasoned to perfection. With its striking presentation and bold flavors, this vegetarian alternative promises a delightful culinary experience that honors the essence of The French Laundry's inventive cuisine.

Serving: Serves: 4
Serving Size: 1/2 cup
Preparation Time: 20 minutes
Ready Time: Total: 1 hour 20 minutes (including chilling time)

Ingredients:
- 4 medium-sized beets, roasted, peeled, and finely diced
- 1 shallot, finely minced
- 2 tablespoons capers, drained and chopped
- 2 tablespoons cornichons, finely chopped
- 1 tablespoon Dijon mustard
- 2 tablespoons extra-virgin olive oil
- 1 tablespoon red wine vinegar
- 2 tablespoons fresh parsley, finely chopped
- Salt and freshly ground black pepper to taste
- Microgreens, for garnish
- Baguette slices or crackers, for serving

Instructions:
1. Prepare the Beets: Preheat the oven to 400°F (200°C). Wash the beets thoroughly and wrap each beet individually in foil. Roast in the oven for about 45-60 minutes, or until tender. Let them cool, then peel and finely dice the beets.
2. Combine Ingredients: In a mixing bowl, combine the diced beets, minced shallot, capers, chopped cornichons, Dijon mustard, olive oil, red wine vinegar, and chopped parsley. Season with salt and pepper to taste. Gently mix until well combined.
3. Chill and Serve: Cover the beet mixture and refrigerate for at least 1 hour to allow the flavors to meld together. When ready to serve, shape the beet tartare using a ring mold for an elegant presentation or simply spoon onto plates. Garnish with microgreens.
4. Serve: Accompany the beet tartare with slices of toasted baguette or your favorite crackers.

Nutrition Information:
(per serving)
- Calories: 120
- Total Fat: 7g
- Saturated Fat: 1g
- Sodium: 270mg
- Total Carbohydrate: 13g
- Dietary Fiber: 3g
- Sugars: 9g
- Protein: 2g

Note: Nutrition information is approximate and may vary based on actual ingredients used.

This Beet "Tartare" recipe is a celebration of flavors and textures, showcasing the brilliance of vegetarian cuisine while paying homage to the artistry of The French Laundry's menu. Enjoy the bold and refreshing taste of this dish, perfect for both casual gatherings and elegant dining experiences.

13. Cauliflower "Panna Cotta"

Indulge your palate in the exquisite world of culinary sophistication with this Cauliflower Panna Cotta, a dish inspired by the renowned menu of Thomas Keller's iconic restaurant, The French Laundry. Elevating the humble cauliflower to new heights, this creamy and velvety dessert is a testament to the artistry and innovation synonymous with Keller's culinary legacy.

Serving: 4 servings
Preparation Time: 20 minutes
Ready Time: 4 hours (including chilling time)

Ingredients:
- 1 small head of cauliflower, chopped
- 1 cup heavy cream
- 1 cup whole milk
- 1/2 cup granulated sugar
- 1 vanilla bean, split and seeds scraped
- 3 gelatin sheets (or 1 envelope gelatin powder)

- Pinch of salt

Instructions:
1. Prepare the Cauliflower:
- Steam the chopped cauliflower until tender.
- In a blender, puree the steamed cauliflower until smooth. Set aside.
2. Infuse the Dairy:
- In a saucepan, combine the heavy cream, whole milk, sugar, vanilla bean seeds, and the split vanilla bean pod.
- Heat the mixture over medium heat until it just begins to simmer, then remove from heat.
3. Bloom the Gelatin:
- If using gelatin sheets, soak them in cold water until softened. If using gelatin powder, follow the package instructions.
- Squeeze excess water from the gelatin sheets and add them to the warm dairy mixture, or add the bloomed gelatin powder. Stir until completely dissolved.
4. Combine Cauliflower Puree:
- Whisk the cauliflower puree into the dairy mixture until well combined. Add a pinch of salt to balance the flavors.
5. Strain the Mixture:
- Strain the mixture through a fine-mesh sieve into a clean bowl, discarding any solids. This step ensures a silky-smooth texture.
6. Pour into Molds:
- Divide the cauliflower panna cotta mixture among four serving molds or ramekins.
7. Chill:
- Refrigerate the molds for at least 4 hours or until set.
8. Unmold and Serve:
- To serve, run a knife around the edge of each mold and dip the bottom briefly in hot water. Invert onto serving plates.

Nutrition Information:
(Per Serving)
- Calories: 320
- Fat: 25g
- Saturated Fat: 15g
- Cholesterol: 90mg
- Sodium: 80mg
- Carbohydrates: 20g

- Sugar: 18g
- Protein: 4g

Experience the symphony of flavors and textures in this Cauliflower Panna Cotta—a sublime tribute to the culinary mastery of Thomas Keller's The French Laundry.

14. Sweet Butter-Poached Maine Lobster

Indulge in the exquisite flavors of Thomas Keller's culinary mastery with our Sweet Butter-Poached Maine Lobster recipe. Inspired by the refined elegance of The French Laundry restaurant, this dish promises a symphony of succulent lobster, rich butter, and delicate sweetness. Elevate your dining experience and embark on a journey of gastronomic delight with this luxurious creation.

Serving: 4 servings
Preparation Time: 20 minutes
Ready Time: 45 minutes

Ingredients:
- 4 Maine lobsters (1-1.5 pounds each)
- 1 cup unsalted butter
- 1 vanilla bean, split and scraped
- 1/4 cup granulated sugar
- 1 teaspoon sea salt
- Zest of 1 lemon
- 1 tablespoon fresh chives, finely chopped (for garnish)

Instructions:
1. Prepare the Lobster:
- Bring a large pot of salted water to boil.
- Quickly blanch the lobsters for 1-2 minutes to loosen the meat. Remove from boiling water and let them cool slightly.
- With a sharp knife, carefully split the lobsters in half lengthwise. Remove the claws and knuckles, cracking them slightly to ease meat removal.
2. Butter Poaching Mixture:
- In a saucepan over low heat, melt the unsalted butter.

- Add the scraped vanilla bean, granulated sugar, sea salt, and lemon zest to the butter. Stir until the sugar dissolves and the flavors meld.
3. Poach the Lobster:
- Preheat your oven to 325°F (163°C).
- Place lobster halves in a baking dish and pour the butter mixture over them, ensuring each piece is generously coated.
- Bake for 20-25 minutes, basting the lobster with the butter sauce every 5 minutes, until the meat is opaque and cooked through.
4. Garnish and Serve:
- Remove lobster from the oven and sprinkle with fresh chives for a burst of color and additional flavor.
- Serve the Sweet Butter-Poached Maine Lobster on a platter, drizzling any remaining butter sauce over the top.

Nutrition Information (per serving):
- Calories: 480
- Protein: 28g
- Fat: 38g
- Carbohydrates: 8g
- Fiber: 0.5g
- Sugar: 7g
- Cholesterol: 185mg
- Sodium: 780mg

Elevate your home cooking with this decadent Sweet Butter-Poached Maine Lobster, inspired by the culinary excellence of The French Laundry. Revel in the divine combination of flavors and textures that make this dish a true celebration of fine dining.

15. Yukon Gold Potato "Levée"

Inspired by the culinary excellence of Thomas Keller's The French Laundry, the Yukon Gold Potato "Levée" is a dish that elevates the humble potato to a level of sophistication that is both comforting and refined. This recipe showcases the versatility of Yukon Gold potatoes, known for their buttery texture and rich flavor, making them the perfect canvas for culinary artistry. The dish is a celebration of simplicity, where each ingredient plays a crucial role in creating a symphony of flavors that will leave a lasting impression on your palate.

Serving: 4 servings
Preparation Time: 20 minutes
Ready Time: 1 hour

Ingredients:
- 4 large Yukon Gold potatoes, peeled and thinly sliced
- 1 cup heavy cream
- 1 cup whole milk
- 2 cloves garlic, minced
- 1 sprig fresh thyme
- 1 bay leaf
- Salt and pepper to taste
- 1 cup Gruyère cheese, grated
- 1/2 cup Parmesan cheese, grated
- Butter for greasing the baking dish

Instructions:
1. Preheat Oven:
Preheat your oven to 375°F (190°C).
2. Prepare Potatoes:
Peel and thinly slice the Yukon Gold potatoes. A mandoline slicer works well for achieving uniform thickness.
3. Make Cream Mixture:
In a saucepan, combine the heavy cream, whole milk, minced garlic, thyme, bay leaf, salt, and pepper. Heat the mixture over medium heat until it simmers. Remove from heat and let it steep for 10 minutes to infuse the flavors.
4. Layer Potatoes:
Butter a baking dish and layer the sliced potatoes evenly.
5. Strain Cream Mixture:
Strain the cream mixture to remove the garlic, thyme, and bay leaf. Pour the infused cream over the layered potatoes.
6. Cheese Layer:
Sprinkle the Gruyère and Parmesan cheeses over the potatoes, ensuring an even distribution.
7. Bake:
Cover the baking dish with aluminum foil and bake in the preheated oven for 30 minutes. After 30 minutes, remove the foil and bake for an

additional 20-30 minutes or until the top is golden brown, and the potatoes are tender.

8. Serve:

Allow the Yukon Gold Potato "Levée" to rest for a few minutes before serving. This dish pairs wonderfully with a fresh green salad or can be enjoyed on its own as a comforting side.

Nutrition Information:
Note: Nutritional values are approximate and may vary based on specific ingredients used.
- Calories per serving: 400
- Total Fat: 25g
- Saturated Fat: 15g
- Trans Fat: 0.5g
- Cholesterol: 80mg
- Sodium: 300mg
- Total Carbohydrates: 35g
- Dietary Fiber: 4g
- Sugars: 3g
- Protein: 12g

Indulge in the luxurious simplicity of this Yukon Gold Potato "Levée," a dish that captures the essence of Thomas Keller's culinary artistry at The French Laundry.

16. "Salad" of Hawaiian Hearts of Peach Palm

Indulge in the vibrant flavors of Hawaii with our Hawaiian Hearts of Peach Palm Salad, inspired by the culinary excellence of Thomas Keller's The French Laundry. This refreshing salad captures the essence of tropical paradise, featuring the delicate hearts of peach palm as the star ingredient. With a symphony of textures and tastes, this dish is a celebration of freshness and innovation, perfect for any occasion.

Serving: 4 servings
Preparation Time: 15 minutes
Ready Time: 20 minutes

Ingredients:

- 2 cups Hawaiian hearts of peach palm, thinly sliced
- 1 cup fresh pineapple chunks
- 1 cup cherry tomatoes, halved
- 1 avocado, diced
- 1/4 cup red onion, finely sliced
- 1/4 cup fresh cilantro, chopped
- 1/4 cup macadamia nuts, toasted and chopped

For the Dressing:
- 3 tablespoons extra virgin olive oil
- 2 tablespoons pineapple juice
- 1 tablespoon lime juice
- 1 teaspoon honey
- Salt and pepper to taste

Instructions:
1. Prepare the Salad:
- In a large salad bowl, combine the sliced Hawaiian hearts of peach palm, fresh pineapple chunks, cherry tomatoes, diced avocado, sliced red onion, and chopped cilantro.
2. Make the Dressing:
- In a small bowl, whisk together the extra virgin olive oil, pineapple juice, lime juice, honey, salt, and pepper until well combined.
3. Assemble the Salad:
- Pour the dressing over the salad ingredients and gently toss to coat evenly.
4. Top with Macadamia Nuts:
- Sprinkle the toasted and chopped macadamia nuts over the salad for a delightful crunch.
5. Serve:
- Divide the salad among four plates, ensuring an even distribution of ingredients.
6. Garnish:
- For a final touch, garnish with additional cilantro and a drizzle of dressing if desired.

Nutrition Information:
- *Note: Nutrition values are approximate and may vary based on specific ingredients and quantities used.*
- Calories: 250 per serving
- Total Fat: 18g

- Saturated Fat: 2g
- Trans Fat: 0g
- Cholesterol: 0mg
- Sodium: 150mg
- Total Carbohydrates: 22g
- Dietary Fiber: 8g
- Sugars: 10g
- Protein: 4g

Enjoy this Hawaiian Hearts of Peach Palm Salad as a vibrant and nutritious addition to your culinary repertoire. It's a taste of paradise in every bite, inspired by the innovative menu of Thomas Keller's The French Laundry.

17. Sauteed Fillet of Gulf Coast Cobia

Elevate your dining experience with this exquisite recipe inspired by the legendary Thomas Keller's The French Laundry restaurant. Indulge in the succulent flavors of Sauteed Fillet of Gulf Coast Cobia, a dish that captures the essence of fine dining and the freshness of Gulf Coast seafood. The simple yet sophisticated preparation ensures that every bite is a celebration of taste and texture.

Serving: 4 servings
Preparation Time: 15 minutes
Ready Time: 30 minutes

Ingredients:
- 4 Gulf Coast Cobia fillets (about 6 ounces each)
- Salt and black pepper, to taste
- 2 tablespoons olive oil
- 2 tablespoons unsalted butter
- 2 cloves garlic, minced
- 1 tablespoon fresh lemon juice
- 1 tablespoon chopped fresh parsley

Instructions:
1. Prepare the Cobia Fillets:
- Pat the Cobia fillets dry with paper towels.

- Season both sides of the fillets with salt and black pepper.
2. Sauté the Fillets:
- In a large skillet, heat olive oil over medium-high heat.
- Place the Cobia fillets in the skillet, skin side down, and cook for 3-4 minutes until the skin is crispy and golden brown.
- Flip the fillets and cook the other side for an additional 2-3 minutes or until the fish is cooked through and flakes easily with a fork.
- Transfer the fillets to a serving platter.
3. Prepare the Sauce:
- In the same skillet, add butter and minced garlic. Sauté for 1-2 minutes until the garlic is fragrant.
- Stir in fresh lemon juice and chopped parsley, cooking for an additional minute.
4. Serve:
- Spoon the garlic and lemon butter sauce over the sautéed Cobia fillets.
5. Garnish and Enjoy:
- Garnish with additional chopped parsley.
- Serve immediately, allowing your guests to savor the freshness of the Gulf Coast Cobia.

Nutrition Information:
(per serving)
- Calories: 320
- Total Fat: 20g
- Saturated Fat: 7g
- Trans Fat: 0g
- Cholesterol: 90mg
- Sodium: 350mg
- Total Carbohydrates: 1g
- Dietary Fiber: 0g
- Sugars: 0g
- Protein: 34g

Delight your palate with the exquisite Sauteed Fillet of Gulf Coast Cobia – a dish that brings the sophistication of The French Laundry into your own kitchen.

18. Slowly Poached Moulard Duck Foie Gras

Indulge in the exquisite world of gourmet cuisine with this decadent recipe inspired by the renowned menu of Thomas Keller's iconic restaurant, The French Laundry. Our Slowly Poached Moulard Duck Foie Gras is a testament to the delicate art of French cooking, where every bite promises a symphony of rich flavors and luxurious textures. Elevate your dining experience with this classic dish that pays homage to the culinary mastery of one of the world's most celebrated chefs.

Serving: 4 servings
Preparation Time: 20 minutes
Ready Time: 24 hours (including chilling time)

Ingredients:
- 4 Moulard Duck Foie Gras lobes, about 8 ounces each
- 1 tablespoon kosher salt
- 1 teaspoon white pepper
- 1/4 cup Sauternes wine
- 1/4 cup Armagnac
- 1 teaspoon pink curing salt (optional)
- 4 cups duck fat, melted
- Baguette slices or brioche, for serving
- Fig or fruit compote, for garnish

Instructions:
1. Prepare the Foie Gras:
- Carefully devein the foie gras lobes, removing any connective tissues.
- Season each lobe with kosher salt and white pepper, ensuring an even distribution.
- In a small bowl, mix the Sauternes wine and Armagnac. Drizzle the mixture over the foie gras, ensuring it is well-coated. Allow the foie gras to marinate in the refrigerator for at least 4 hours or overnight.
2. Preheat the Oven:
- Preheat your oven to 180°F (82°C).
3. Poach the Foie Gras:
- Place the marinated foie gras in a heatproof dish. If using, sprinkle the pink curing salt over the foie gras.
- Pour the melted duck fat over the foie gras, ensuring it is completely submerged.
- Cover the dish with aluminum foil and place it in the preheated oven. Slowly poach the foie gras for 2 to 3 hours until it is set but still creamy.

4. Chill and Set:
- Allow the poached foie gras to cool to room temperature before transferring it to the refrigerator.
- Chill the foie gras for at least 24 hours to allow the flavors to meld and the texture to set.

5. Serve:
- Remove the foie gras from the refrigerator about 30 minutes before serving to bring it to a spreadable consistency.
- Serve the Slowly Poached Moulard Duck Foie Gras on slices of toasted baguette or brioche.
- Garnish with a dollop of fig or fruit compote for a delightful contrast of flavors.

Nutrition Information:
Note: Nutrition information is approximate and may vary based on specific ingredients used.
- Calories per serving: 450
- Fat: 40g
- Saturated Fat: 15g
- Cholesterol: 300mg
- Sodium: 750mg
- Carbohydrates: 5g
- Protein: 12g

Indulge in the opulence of this Slowly Poached Moulard Duck Foie Gras, a dish that epitomizes the sophisticated charm of French culinary traditions. Elevate your dining experience and savor the luxurious textures and flavors inspired by the culinary genius of Thomas Keller's The French Laundry.

19. Carnaroli Risotto Biologico

Embark on a culinary journey inspired by the renowned Thomas Keller's The French Laundry restaurant with this exquisite dish - Carnaroli Risotto Biologico. Elevate your dining experience with the finest organic Carnaroli rice, meticulously prepared to perfection. The rich flavors and creamy texture of this classic Italian dish will transport you to the heart of fine dining, encapsulating the essence of Keller's culinary philosophy.

Serving: 4 servings
Preparation Time: 15 minutes
Ready Time: 30 minutes

Ingredients:
- 1 cup organic Carnaroli rice
- 4 cups organic vegetable broth, heated
- 1/2 cup dry white wine
- 1/2 cup organic Parmesan cheese, grated
- 2 tablespoons organic unsalted butter
- 1 small organic onion, finely chopped
- 2 cloves organic garlic, minced
- Salt and pepper to taste
- Fresh organic parsley, chopped (for garnish)

Instructions:
1. In a heavy-bottomed pan, melt 1 tablespoon of butter over medium heat. Add the chopped onion and garlic, sautéing until translucent.
2. Add the Carnaroli rice to the pan, stirring to coat the grains with the butter and allowing them to toast slightly, enhancing their nutty flavor.
3. Pour in the white wine, stirring continuously until it's mostly absorbed by the rice.
4. Begin adding the heated vegetable broth, one ladle at a time, allowing the rice to absorb the liquid before adding the next ladle. Continue this process until the rice is creamy and cooked to al dente texture.
5. Stir in the remaining butter and grated Parmesan cheese, ensuring a velvety finish. Season with salt and pepper to taste.
6. Remove the risotto from heat and let it rest for a couple of minutes. This allows the flavors to meld and the dish to reach its optimal creamy consistency.
7. Serve the Carnaroli Risotto Biologico in individual plates, garnished with fresh chopped parsley for a burst of color and flavor.

Nutrition Information:
(Per Serving)
- Calories: 380
- Protein: 8g
- Fat: 12g
- Carbohydrates: 55g
- Fiber: 2g

- Sugar: 1g
- Sodium: 800mg

Indulge in the timeless elegance of Carnaroli Risotto Biologico, a dish that pays homage to the culinary excellence of Thomas Keller's The French Laundry.

20. Chatham Bay Cod "Brandade"

Inspired by the culinary excellence of Thomas Keller's The French Laundry restaurant, this Chatham Bay Cod Brandade is a sublime interpretation of classic French flavors. The dish features the delicate and flaky Chatham Bay Cod, masterfully blended with creamy potatoes and infused with aromatic herbs. Elevate your dining experience with this sophisticated and comforting brandade, a dish that seamlessly combines tradition with innovation.

Serving: 4 servings
Preparation Time: 20 minutes
Ready Time: 45 minutes

Ingredients:
- 1 lb Chatham Bay Cod fillets, skinless and boneless
- 1 lb Yukon Gold potatoes, peeled and diced
- 1 cup whole milk
- 1/2 cup extra virgin olive oil
- 4 cloves garlic, minced
- 2 sprigs fresh thyme
- 1 bay leaf
- Salt and pepper to taste
- Chopped fresh parsley for garnish

Instructions:
1. Prepare the Cod: In a medium-sized saucepan, combine the cod fillets, milk, thyme, and bay leaf. Gently simmer over low heat for 10-15 minutes or until the cod is easily flaked with a fork. Remove from heat, discard the herbs, and set aside.
2. Boil Potatoes: In a separate pot, boil the diced potatoes until tender. Drain and mash them while they are still warm.

3. Blend the Brandade: In a food processor, combine the flaked cod and mashed potatoes. Pulse until the mixture is smooth and creamy. Add olive oil gradually, blending continuously, until the brandade reaches a silky consistency.
4. Sauté Garlic: In a pan, heat a tablespoon of olive oil over medium heat. Add minced garlic and sauté until fragrant, taking care not to brown it.
5. Incorporate Garlic into Brandade: Add the sautéed garlic to the cod and potato mixture. Blend again until well combined. Season with salt and pepper to taste.
6. Warm Brandade: Return the brandade to a low heat, stirring continuously until warmed through.
7. Serve: Spoon the Chatham Bay Cod Brandade onto plates, drizzle with extra olive oil, and garnish with chopped fresh parsley.

Nutrition Information:
(Per Serving)
- Calories: 380
- Protein: 22g
- Carbohydrates: 25g
- Fat: 20g
- Fiber: 3g

Indulge in the rich flavors of this Chatham Bay Cod Brandade, a tribute to the culinary finesse of Thomas Keller's iconic restaurant, The French Laundry.

21. Nantes Carrot "Vichyssoise"

This Nantes Carrot Vichyssoise is a tribute to the exquisite flavors celebrated at Thomas Keller's The French Laundry. Inspired by the restaurant's commitment to culinary excellence, this velvety soup combines the sweetness of Nantes carrots with the classic French touch of a Vichyssoise. It's a harmonious blend of elegance and simplicity, perfect for indulging in refined flavors.

Serving: 4 servings
Preparation time: 15 minutes
Ready time: 1 hour 30 minutes

Ingredients:
- 1 pound Nantes carrots, peeled and chopped
- 1 large leek, white and light green parts only, sliced
- 2 tablespoons unsalted butter
- 1 medium onion, chopped
- 2 garlic cloves, minced
- 2 cups chicken or vegetable broth
- 1 cup whole milk
- 1 cup heavy cream
- Salt and pepper, to taste
- Fresh chives, chopped (for garnish)

Instructions:
1. Prepare the Vegetables: In a large pot, melt the butter over medium heat. Add the chopped onion, sliced leek, and minced garlic. Sauté until the vegetables soften, about 5 minutes.
2. Cook the Carrots: Add the chopped Nantes carrots to the pot and continue to cook for another 5 minutes, stirring occasionally.
3. Simmer with Broth: Pour in the chicken or vegetable broth, ensuring it covers the vegetables. Bring the mixture to a boil, then reduce the heat to low. Cover and simmer for 30-40 minutes or until the carrots are tender.
4. Blend the Soup: Once the carrots are soft, remove the pot from heat and let it cool slightly. Use a blender or an immersion blender to purée the mixture until smooth.
5. Make it Creamy: Return the puréed mixture to the pot over low heat. Stir in the whole milk and heavy cream, allowing the soup to heat through without boiling. Season with salt and pepper to taste.
6. Serve: Ladle the Nantes Carrot Vichyssoise into bowls. Garnish with fresh chopped chives for an added layer of flavor and visual appeal.

Nutrition Information: (per serving)
Note: Nutritional values may vary based on specific ingredients used.
- Calories: 320
- Fat: 25g
- Carbohydrates: 20g
- Protein: 5g
- Fiber: 5g

This Nantes Carrot Vichyssoise is a delightfully rich and creamy soup, embodying the essence of French cuisine. Enjoy its luxurious taste and the warmth it brings with each comforting spoonful.

22. Freshwater Eel "Savarin"

A culinary homage to the refined elegance of Thomas Keller's The French Laundry, this "Freshwater Eel Savarin" encapsulates the essence of fine dining. Delicately balancing flavors, this dish pays tribute to the restaurant's commitment to excellence and innovation.

Serving: 4 servings
Preparation time: 30 minutes
Ready time: Approximately 2 hours

Ingredients:
- 2 cups all-purpose flour
- 1/4 cup granulated sugar
- 1 tablespoon active dry yeast
- 1/2 teaspoon salt
- 3/4 cup warm milk
- 3 large eggs
- 1/4 cup unsalted butter, softened
- 2 tablespoons honey
- 1 tablespoon finely grated lemon zest
- 1 cup sliced freshwater eel fillets
- 1/4 cup Japanese mirin
- 2 tablespoons soy sauce
- 1 tablespoon rice vinegar
- 1 tablespoon sesame oil
- 1 teaspoon grated ginger
- 1 teaspoon cornstarch
- Chives or microgreens for garnish (optional)

Instructions:
1. Prepare the Savarin Dough:
- In a large mixing bowl, combine the flour, sugar, yeast, and salt.
- Warm the milk slightly and whisk in 2 eggs.

- Gradually pour the milk mixture into the dry ingredients, stirring continuously until a smooth, elastic dough forms.
- Incorporate the softened butter, honey, and lemon zest. Knead the dough until it becomes soft and pliable.
- Cover the bowl with a clean towel and allow the dough to rise in a warm place until it doubles in size, approximately 1 hour.

2. Cook the Freshwater Eel:
- In a saucepan, combine the mirin, soy sauce, rice vinegar, sesame oil, grated ginger, and cornstarch. Heat the mixture over medium heat, stirring until it thickens slightly.
- Add the sliced freshwater eel fillets to the saucepan and cook gently until the eel is just tender and glazed with the sauce. Set aside.

3. Bake the Savarin:
- Preheat the oven to 350°F (175°C).
- Grease a Savarin mold or a ring mold and place it on a baking sheet.
- Punch down the risen dough and transfer it to the prepared mold, shaping it evenly.
- Let the dough rise again for about 15-20 minutes.
- Beat the remaining egg and brush it gently over the surface of the dough.
- Bake in the preheated oven for 20-25 minutes or until golden brown and cooked through.

4. Assemble:
- Once the Savarin is baked and cooled, carefully remove it from the mold.
- Slice the Savarin horizontally into individual servings.
- Place a generous portion of the cooked eel on top of each slice.
- Drizzle any remaining glaze over the eel.
- Garnish with chives or microgreens if desired.

Nutrition Information: *Nutritional information may vary based on specific ingredients used and serving sizes. A rough estimate per serving would be approximately 350-400 calories, 15g fat, 40g carbohydrates, 15g protein.*

This Freshwater Eel Savarin is a sophisticated dish that showcases the artistry and finesse inspired by the renowned culinary legacy of The French Laundry. Enjoy the harmony of flavors and textures in each bite, reminiscent of Keller's dedication to culinary perfection.

23. Herb-Crusted Sautéed Fillet of Pacific Sturgeon

Indulge in the culinary brilliance of Thomas Keller's The French Laundry with this exquisite Herb-Crusted Sautéed Fillet of Pacific Sturgeon. This dish embodies the essence of finesse and flavor, showcasing a harmonious blend of herbs that elevate the delicate taste of Pacific sturgeon. Perfectly seared to a golden crust, each bite promises a symphony of textures and tastes reminiscent of the renowned restaurant's exquisite offerings.

Serving: Serves 4
Preparation Time: 20 minutes
Ready Time: 30 minutes

Ingredients:
- 4 Pacific sturgeon fillets (6-8 ounces each)
- 2 tablespoons olive oil
- Salt and freshly ground black pepper to taste
- 1 cup breadcrumbs (preferably Panko)
- 2 tablespoons fresh parsley, finely chopped
- 1 tablespoon fresh chives, finely chopped
- 1 tablespoon fresh thyme leaves
- Zest of 1 lemon
- 2 cloves garlic, minced
- 2 tablespoons unsalted butter

Instructions:
1. Prepare the Herb Crust: In a mixing bowl, combine breadcrumbs, parsley, chives, thyme, lemon zest, minced garlic, salt, and pepper. Mix thoroughly to create the herb crust mixture.
2. Season the Sturgeon: Pat dry the sturgeon fillets and season both sides generously with salt and pepper.
3. Coat with Herb Mixture: Press the herb crust mixture onto both sides of each sturgeon fillet, ensuring an even coating.
4. Sear the Fillets: Heat olive oil in a large skillet over medium-high heat. Once hot, carefully add the sturgeon fillets to the skillet. Sauté for about 3-4 minutes on each side until the crust becomes golden and the fish is cooked through. Adjust timing based on fillet thickness.

5. Add Butter for Flavor: During the last minute of cooking, add butter to the skillet. Tilt the skillet and spoon the melted butter over the fillets continuously for added richness.

6. Serve: Remove the fillets from the skillet and place them on serving plates. Drizzle any remaining butter from the skillet over the fillets for added flavor.

Nutrition Information (per serving):
Please note, these values are approximate and may vary based on specific ingredients and portion sizes.
- Calories: 320
- Total Fat: 16g
- Saturated Fat: 5g
- Cholesterol: 90mg
- Sodium: 350mg
- Total Carbohydrates: 9g
- Dietary Fiber: 1g
- Sugars: 1g
- Protein: 34g

This elegant Herb-Crusted Sautéed Fillet of Pacific Sturgeon encapsulates the essence of fine dining and is perfect for an exquisite meal reminiscent of the culinary delights of The French Laundry.

24. Sweet Butter-Poached Maine Lobster Tail

Indulge your senses in the exquisite world of fine dining with this Sweet Butter-Poached Maine Lobster Tail, a culinary masterpiece inspired by the legendary menu of Thomas Keller's iconic restaurant, The French Laundry. Elevating the essence of simplicity, this dish captures the essence of luxurious dining and brings the sophistication of French cuisine to your own table.

Serving: 4 servings
Preparation Time: 20 minutes
Ready Time: 40 minutes

Ingredients:
- 4 Maine lobster tails, shells intact

- 1 cup unsalted butter
- 2 tablespoons granulated sugar
- 1 vanilla bean, split and scraped
- 1 teaspoon sea salt
- Zest of 1 lemon
- Fresh chives, finely chopped (for garnish)

Instructions:
1. Prepare the Lobster Tails:
- Using kitchen shears, carefully cut through the top of each lobster shell, exposing the meat without detaching it completely.
- Gently lift the lobster meat and place it on top of the shell, leaving the tail end attached.
2. Poaching Liquid:
- In a medium saucepan, melt the unsalted butter over low heat.
- Add the granulated sugar, vanilla bean seeds, and sea salt to the melted butter, stirring until the sugar is dissolved.
- Stir in the lemon zest, infusing the butter with a subtle citrus flavor.
3. Poaching the Lobster Tails:
- Preheat your oven to 325°F (163°C).
- Place the lobster tails in a baking dish and pour the prepared poaching liquid over them, ensuring each tail is generously coated.
- Bake in the preheated oven for 15-20 minutes or until the lobster meat is opaque and cooked through.
4. Basting:
- Every 5 minutes, baste the lobster tails with the poaching liquid, ensuring they remain moist and flavorful.
5. Serve:
- Carefully transfer the lobster tails to serving plates, drizzling them with the remaining poaching liquid.
- Garnish with fresh chives for a burst of color and additional depth of flavor.

Nutrition Information:
(per serving)
- Calories: 380
- Protein: 20g
- Fat: 30g
- Carbohydrates: 5g
- Fiber: 0.5g

- Sugar: 3g
- Sodium: 650mg

Indulge in the extraordinary with this Sweet Butter-Poached Maine Lobster Tail, a testament to the culinary brilliance that defines Thomas Keller's The French Laundry. Each bite is a symphony of flavors, showcasing the delicate sweetness of lobster enveloped in the richness of vanilla-infused butter—a true delight for the senses.

25. "Tongue in Cheek" Creekstone Farm Beef Cheeks

Delve into the exquisite world of Thomas Keller's culinary mastery with our inspired dish, "Tongue in Cheek" Creekstone Farm Beef Cheeks. This recipe pays homage to the artistry found in the iconic menu of The French Laundry restaurant. Slow-cooked to perfection, Creekstone Farm Beef Cheeks showcase the rich and succulent flavors that define Keller's culinary philosophy. Elevate your dining experience with this gourmet delight that captures the essence of fine French cuisine.

Serving: 4 servings
Preparation Time: 20 minutes
Ready Time: 6 hours

Ingredients:
- 4 Creekstone Farm beef cheeks
- Salt and black pepper, to taste
- 2 tablespoons olive oil
- 1 onion, finely chopped
- 2 carrots, diced
- 3 cloves garlic, minced
- 1 cup red wine
- 2 cups beef broth
- 2 sprigs fresh thyme
- 2 bay leaves
- 1 tablespoon tomato paste
- Mashed potatoes or creamy polenta, for serving (optional)
- Chopped fresh parsley, for garnish

Instructions:
1. Preheat your oven to 325°F (160°C).
2. Season the Creekstone Farm beef cheeks generously with salt and black pepper.
3. In a large ovenproof pot or Dutch oven, heat the olive oil over medium-high heat. Sear the beef cheeks on all sides until browned. Remove the cheeks and set them aside.
4. In the same pot, add the chopped onion, diced carrots, and minced garlic. Sauté until the vegetables are softened.
5. Pour in the red wine, scraping the bottom of the pot to release any flavorful bits. Allow the wine to simmer and reduce by half.
6. Return the beef cheeks to the pot. Add beef broth, thyme, bay leaves, and tomato paste. Bring the mixture to a simmer.
7. Cover the pot and transfer it to the preheated oven. Allow the beef cheeks to braise for about 4-5 hours or until they are fork-tender.
8. Once done, remove the pot from the oven. Discard the thyme sprigs and bay leaves.
9. Serve the Creekstone Farm Beef Cheeks over a bed of mashed potatoes or creamy polenta, if desired. Garnish with chopped fresh parsley.

Nutrition Information:
(Per serving)
- Calories: 450
- Protein: 30g
- Fat: 25g
- Carbohydrates: 15g
- Fiber: 3g
- Sugar: 4g
- Sodium: 800mg

Indulge in the luxurious flavors of this "Tongue in Cheek" Creekstone Farm Beef Cheeks recipe, a sublime representation of the culinary excellence celebrated at The French Laundry.

26. "Chaud-Froid" of Poularde

Chaud-Froid of Poularde is a culinary masterpiece inspired by the exquisite menu of Thomas Keller's renowned restaurant, The French

Laundry. This dish seamlessly blends classic French techniques with modern innovation, creating a symphony of flavors and textures. Chaud-Froid, translating to "hot-cold" in French, refers to the unique preparation method where a protein, in this case, succulent poularde (chicken), is poached to perfection, then delicately coated with a velvety chaud-froid sauce, resulting in a dish that is as visually stunning as it is delicious.

Serving: Ideal for an intimate dinner or a special occasion, this dish serves 4.
Preparation Time: 30 minutes
Ready Time: 2 hours

Ingredients:
- 1 whole poularde (approximately 4 pounds)
- 1 onion, roughly chopped
- 2 carrots, peeled and sliced
- 2 celery stalks, chopped
- 1 leek, cleaned and sliced
- 1 bouquet garni (a bundle of herbs such as thyme, parsley, and bay leaves)
- Salt and pepper to taste

For the Chaud-Froid Sauce:
- 2 cups chicken stock
- 1 cup heavy cream
- 2 tablespoons gelatin
- Salt and white pepper to taste
- Lemon juice, to taste

For Garnish:
- Fresh herbs (chervil, tarragon, or chives)
- Edible flowers (optional)

Instructions:
1. In a large pot, bring water to a simmer. Add the poularde, onion, carrots, celery, leek, bouquet garni, salt, and pepper. Simmer gently for about 1.5 to 2 hours until the poularde is cooked through.
2. Remove the poularde from the pot and let it cool. Once cooled, carefully remove the meat from the bones and set aside.
3. Strain the poaching liquid to use as a base for the chaud-froid sauce.

4. In a saucepan, combine chicken stock and gelatin. Allow the gelatin to bloom for a few minutes.
5. Place the saucepan over low heat and stir until the gelatin dissolves. Add the strained poaching liquid and heavy cream. Continue to cook, stirring constantly, until the mixture thickens.
6. Season the chaud-froid sauce with salt, white pepper, and a touch of lemon juice for brightness. Allow the sauce to cool.
7. Once the sauce has cooled to room temperature, coat the poached poularde with a thin layer of the chaud-froid sauce.
8. Refrigerate the poularde until the chaud-froid sauce sets.
9. Before serving, garnish with fresh herbs and edible flowers for an elegant presentation.

Nutrition Information:
(Note: Nutritional values may vary based on specific ingredients and portion sizes.)
- Calories per serving: XXX
- Protein: XXXg
- Fat: XXXg
- Carbohydrates: XXXg
- Fiber: XXXg
- Sugar: XXXg
- Sodium: XXXmg

Indulge in the culinary artistry of Chaud-Froid of Poularde—a dish that pays homage to the sophisticated flavors and techniques championed by Thomas Keller at The French Laundry. This recipe invites you to elevate your culinary skills and create a dining experience that is nothing short of extraordinary.

27. Slow-Roasted Liberty Duck Breast

Elevate your culinary experience with this exquisite recipe inspired by the legendary menu of Thomas Keller's iconic restaurant, The French Laundry. The Slow-Roasted Liberty Duck Breast is a masterpiece that combines the rich flavors of Liberty duck with a methodical slow-roasting process, resulting in a succulent and flavorful dish that pays homage to Keller's commitment to perfection.

Serving: 4 servings
Preparation Time: 20 minutes
Ready Time: 2 hours and 30 minutes

Ingredients:
- 4 Liberty duck breasts, skin-on
- Salt and freshly ground black pepper
- 2 tablespoons olive oil
- 4 sprigs of fresh thyme
- 4 cloves garlic, peeled and crushed
- 1 cup red wine
- 1 cup chicken broth
- 2 tablespoons unsalted butter

Instructions:
1. Preheat the Oven: Preheat your oven to 300°F (150°C).
2. Score the Duck Skin: Using a sharp knife, score the duck skin in a crosshatch pattern. Be careful not to cut into the meat.
3. Season the Duck: Season both sides of the duck breasts with salt and freshly ground black pepper.
4. Sear the Duck: In an oven-safe skillet, heat olive oil over medium-high heat. Place the duck breasts, skin-side down, and sear until the skin is golden brown and crispy. Flip the breasts and sear the other side for a few minutes.
5. Add Aromatics: Add thyme sprigs and crushed garlic to the skillet. Allow them to infuse their flavors into the duck.
6. Deglaze with Red Wine: Pour in the red wine, scraping the bottom of the pan to release any flavorful bits. Allow the wine to reduce by half.
7. Add Chicken Broth: Pour in the chicken broth, and bring the liquid to a simmer.
8. Slow Roast in the Oven: Transfer the skillet to the preheated oven. Slow-roast the duck for about 2 hours or until the internal temperature reaches 145°F (63°C).
9. Rest and Finish: Once done, remove the duck from the oven and let it rest for 10 minutes. Slice each breast into elegant portions.
10. Make the Sauce: In a saucepan, melt unsalted butter over low heat. Pour in the pan juices from the duck skillet and whisk until combined. This will create a luscious sauce to drizzle over the duck.
11. Serve: Plate the duck slices and generously drizzle the sauce over them. Garnish with fresh thyme leaves for a final touch.

Nutrition Information:
(Note: Nutrition information is approximate and may vary based on specific ingredients used.)
- Calories per serving: 400
- Protein: 25g
- Fat: 30g
- Carbohydrates: 2g
- Fiber: 0g
- Sugar: 0g
- Sodium: 500mg

28. Alaskan King Crab "Cassoulet"

Indulge in the luxurious flavors of the sea with this exquisite Alaskan King Crab Cassoulet, inspired by the culinary finesse of Thomas Keller's renowned The French Laundry restaurant. This dish elevates the succulent Alaskan King Crab to new heights, combining it with the rustic charm of a traditional cassoulet. The result is a symphony of rich flavors and textures that will transport your taste buds to the heart of culinary excellence.

Serving: Serves 4
Preparation Time: 30 minutes
Ready Time: 2 hours

Ingredients:
- 2 lbs Alaskan King Crab legs and claws, pre-cooked
- 1 cup dried Great Northern beans, soaked overnight
- 1 lb pork belly, cut into 1-inch cubes
- 4 duck confit legs
- 1 onion, finely chopped
- 2 carrots, peeled and diced
- 4 cloves garlic, minced
- 2 cups chicken stock
- 1 can (14 oz) crushed tomatoes
- 1 bouquet garni (a bundle of fresh thyme, parsley, and bay leaves tied together)

- 1 cup breadcrumbs
- Salt and black pepper to taste
- Chopped fresh parsley for garnish

Instructions:
1. Prepare the Beans:
- Drain the soaked Great Northern beans and rinse them under cold water.
- In a large pot, cover the beans with water and bring to a boil.
- Reduce the heat, cover, and simmer until the beans are just tender (about 30 minutes).
- Drain and set aside.

2. Cook the Meats:
- In a large ovenproof casserole dish, sauté the pork belly until golden brown.
- Add the chopped onions, carrots, and minced garlic. Cook until the vegetables are softened.
- Nestle the duck confit legs into the mixture and add the pre-cooked Alaskan King Crab legs and claws.

3. Build the Cassoulet:
- Pour in the chicken stock and crushed tomatoes.
- Add the cooked beans to the pot and tuck the bouquet garni into the mixture.
- Season with salt and black pepper to taste.
- Bring the cassoulet to a simmer, then cover and transfer it to a preheated oven at 350°F (175°C).

4. Bake to Perfection:
- Allow the cassoulet to bake for approximately 1.5 to 2 hours or until the flavors meld and the top forms a golden crust.
- Sprinkle breadcrumbs over the top during the last 30 minutes of baking for added texture.

5. Serve with Elegance:
- Once out of the oven, let the cassoulet rest for a few minutes.
- Garnish with chopped fresh parsley before serving.

Nutrition Information:
(per serving)
- Calories: 750
- Protein: 45g
- Carbohydrates: 40g

- Fat: 45g
- Fiber: 10g

Experience the opulence of Alaskan King Crab in this Thomas Keller-inspired cassoulet—an homage to the culinary mastery of The French Laundry. Indulge in every bite of this sumptuous dish that marries the sea's bounty with the rustic charm of a classic cassoulet.

29. Herb-Grilled Saddle of Elysian Fields Farm Lamb

Indulge in the culinary opulence inspired by the renowned Thomas Keller's The French Laundry restaurant with our exquisite Herb-Grilled Saddle of Elysian Fields Farm Lamb. This dish is a testament to the artistry of flavors, marrying the pristine quality of Elysian Fields Farm lamb with a medley of fresh herbs, creating a symphony of tastes that will transport your palate to new heights. Elevate your dining experience with this sophisticated recipe that pays homage to the culinary excellence synonymous with The French Laundry.

Serving: 4 servings
Preparation Time: 20 minutes
Ready Time: 2 hours (including marination)

Ingredients:
- 1 Elysian Fields Farm lamb saddle (about 2-3 pounds)
- 4 cloves garlic, minced
- 1 tablespoon fresh rosemary, finely chopped
- 1 tablespoon fresh thyme, finely chopped
- 1 tablespoon fresh parsley, finely chopped
- 1 tablespoon Dijon mustard
- 2 tablespoons extra-virgin olive oil
- Salt and black pepper, to taste

Instructions:
1. Prep the Lamb:
- Preheat your grill to medium-high heat.
- Place the lamb saddle on a clean surface. Pat it dry with paper towels.
- Season the lamb generously with salt and black pepper.

2. Prepare the Herb Marinade:
- In a small bowl, combine the minced garlic, chopped rosemary, thyme, parsley, Dijon mustard, and extra-virgin olive oil.
- Mix the ingredients well to form a cohesive herb marinade.

3. Marinate the Lamb:
- Rub the herb marinade all over the lamb saddle, ensuring it's evenly coated.
- Allow the lamb to marinate for at least 1-2 hours in the refrigerator. This step enhances the flavors and tenderness of the meat.

4. Grill the Lamb:
- Remove the lamb from the refrigerator and let it come to room temperature for about 30 minutes.
- Preheat the grill to medium-high heat.
- Grill the lamb for approximately 15-20 minutes, turning occasionally, or until the internal temperature reaches your desired doneness (145°F/63°C for medium-rare).

5. Rest and Slice:
- Allow the grilled lamb to rest for 10 minutes before slicing. This ensures the juices redistribute, keeping the meat moist and flavorful.

6. Serve:
- Slice the lamb into thick, succulent portions.
- Arrange on a platter and drizzle with any remaining herb marinade for an extra burst of flavor.
- Serve alongside your favorite seasonal vegetables or a light salad.

Nutrition Information:
Note: Nutritional values may vary based on specific cuts of lamb and additional sides.
- Calories per serving: Approximately 400 kcal
- Protein: 30g
- Fat: 28g
- Carbohydrates: 2g
- Fiber: 1g
- Sugar: 0g
- Sodium: 400mg

Immerse yourself in the culinary elegance of The French Laundry with this Herb-Grilled Saddle of Elysian Fields Farm Lamb, a dish that epitomizes the artful combination of simplicity and sophistication. Enjoy the gastronomic journey!

30. Roasted Elysian Fields Farm Baby Lamb

Indulge in the culinary elegance inspired by the legendary Thomas Keller's The French Laundry with our Roasted Elysian Fields Farm Baby Lamb. This exquisite dish captures the essence of fine dining, combining premium ingredients and meticulous preparation to elevate your dining experience. The succulent flavors of tender lamb, perfectly roasted to perfection, will transport you to a realm of gastronomic bliss. Let your taste buds embark on a journey of sophistication with this delightful creation.

Serving: 4 servings
Preparation Time: 30 minutes
Ready Time: 2 hours (including marination and roasting)

Ingredients:
- 1 Elysian Fields Farm baby lamb, approximately 4-5 pounds
- 4 cloves garlic, minced
- 2 tablespoons fresh rosemary, finely chopped
- 1 tablespoon fresh thyme leaves
- 1 teaspoon Dijon mustard
- 1/4 cup extra virgin olive oil
- Salt and black pepper, to taste

Instructions:
1. Preheat the Oven:
Preheat your oven to 375°F (190°C).
2. Prepare the Marinade:
In a small bowl, combine minced garlic, chopped rosemary, thyme leaves, Dijon mustard, and extra virgin olive oil. Mix well to form a smooth marinade.
3. Marinate the Lamb:
Place the Elysian Fields Farm baby lamb in a roasting pan. Generously season with salt and black pepper. Rub the lamb with the prepared marinade, ensuring an even coating. Allow it to marinate for at least 30 minutes to let the flavors infuse.
4. Roasting:

Roast the marinated lamb in the preheated oven for about 1 hour and 30 minutes or until the internal temperature reaches 135°F (57°C) for medium-rare. Baste the lamb with its own juices every 30 minutes to enhance tenderness.

5. Resting Period:

Once roasted, let the lamb rest for 15 minutes before carving. This allows the juices to redistribute, ensuring a moist and flavorful result.

6. Carving:

Carve the lamb into slices, and arrange on a serving platter. Drizzle any remaining pan juices over the slices for an added burst of flavor.

Nutrition Information:
- *Calories:* 450 per serving
- *Protein:* 30g
- *Carbohydrates:* 1g
- *Fat:* 36g
- *Cholesterol:* 120mg
- *Sodium:* 400mg

Delight in the symphony of tastes and textures with this Roasted Elysian Fields Farm Baby Lamb, a culinary masterpiece inspired by the brilliance of Thomas Keller's iconic restaurant, The French Laundry.

31. Pave of Kindai Maguro Tuna

Elevate your culinary experience with this exquisite Pave of Kindai Maguro Tuna inspired by the legendary Thomas Keller's The French Laundry restaurant. Kindai Maguro, renowned for its sustainability and unparalleled quality, takes center stage in this dish. Delicate in flavor yet rich in texture, this recipe celebrates the artistry of fine dining in the comfort of your own home.

Serving: 4 servings
Preparation Time: 20 minutes
Ready Time: 1 hour

Ingredients:
- 1 lb Kindai Maguro Tuna, sashimi grade
- 2 tablespoons sesame oil

- 1 tablespoon soy sauce
- 1 tablespoon mirin
- 1 teaspoon grated ginger
- 1 teaspoon wasabi paste
- 1 tablespoon black and white sesame seeds, toasted
- Fresh chives, finely chopped, for garnish
- Microgreens, for garnish
- Sea salt and black pepper, to taste

Instructions:
1. Begin by slicing the Kindai Maguro Tuna into 1-inch thick rectangular pieces. Season each piece with sea salt and black pepper.
2. In a small bowl, whisk together sesame oil, soy sauce, mirin, grated ginger, and wasabi paste to create a flavorful marinade.
3. Place the tuna slices in a shallow dish and pour the marinade over them, ensuring each piece is well-coated. Allow the tuna to marinate for at least 30 minutes in the refrigerator.
4. While the tuna is marinating, toast the black and white sesame seeds in a dry pan over medium heat until fragrant. Set aside for later use.
5. Preheat a grill or grill pan over medium-high heat. Grill the marinated tuna for about 30 seconds on each side, or until the edges are lightly seared, leaving the center raw.
6. Once grilled, transfer the tuna to a cutting board and let it rest for a few minutes. Slice the tuna into thin, even pieces.
7. Arrange the tuna slices on serving plates, sprinkle with the toasted sesame seeds, and garnish with fresh chives and microgreens.
8. Serve immediately, offering additional soy sauce and wasabi on the side for dipping.

Nutrition Information (per serving):
- Calories: 250
- Protein: 30g
- Fat: 12g
- Carbohydrates: 5g
- Fiber: 1g
- Sugar: 2g
- Sodium: 500mg

Indulge in the sophistication of The French Laundry's influence with this Pave of Kindai Maguro Tuna, a dish that beautifully melds flavors, textures, and culinary finesse.

32. Sauteed Fillet of John Dory

Celebrate the artistry of culinary excellence with this exquisite recipe inspired by the legendary Thomas Keller's The French Laundry restaurant. Sauteed Fillet of John Dory, a dish that embodies the perfect balance of flavors and textures, promises to elevate your dining experience to unparalleled heights. Immerse yourself in the culinary mastery that defines The French Laundry and savor the essence of fine dining with this meticulously crafted recipe.

Serving: 4 servings
Preparation Time: 20 minutes
Ready Time: 30 minutes

Ingredients:
- 4 John Dory fillets (6 ounces each)
- 1/4 cup all-purpose flour
- Salt and pepper to taste
- 2 tablespoons olive oil
- 2 tablespoons unsalted butter
- 2 cloves garlic, minced
- 1/4 cup dry white wine
- 1/2 cup chicken or vegetable broth
- 1 tablespoon lemon juice
- 1 tablespoon capers, drained
- 2 tablespoons fresh parsley, chopped

Instructions:
1. Prepare the John Dory Fillets:
- Pat the fillets dry with paper towels.
- In a shallow dish, combine flour, salt, and pepper.
- Dredge each fillet in the flour mixture, shaking off excess.
2. Sauté the Fillets:
- In a large skillet, heat olive oil over medium-high heat.
- Add the fillets and cook for 3-4 minutes per side, or until golden brown and cooked through.
- Transfer fillets to a plate and cover with foil to keep warm.

3. Prepare the Sauce:
- In the same skillet, melt butter over medium heat.
- Add minced garlic and sauté for 1 minute until fragrant.
- Pour in white wine and deglaze the pan, scraping up any browned bits.
- Stir in broth, lemon juice, and capers. Simmer for 2-3 minutes.

4. Finish the Dish:
- Return the cooked fillets to the skillet, spooning the sauce over them.
- Cook for an additional 2 minutes, allowing the fillets to absorb the flavors.

5. Garnish and Serve:
- Sprinkle chopped parsley over the fillets before serving.
- Plate the fillets and drizzle with the savory sauce.

Nutrition Information:
(Per serving)
- Calories: 320
- Total Fat: 18g
- Saturated Fat: 6g
- Cholesterol: 70mg
- Sodium: 420mg
- Total Carbohydrates: 12g
- Dietary Fiber: 1g
- Sugars: 0.5g
- Protein: 26g

Indulge in the sophistication of The French Laundry with this Sauteed Fillet of John Dory, a dish that captures the essence of culinary excellence in every bite. Elevate your dining experience with this masterpiece inspired by Thomas Keller's renowned restaurant.

33. Brandt Beef Short Rib "Bourguignon"

Indulge in the sumptuous flavors of Thomas Keller's culinary mastery with our exquisite "Brandt Beef Short Rib Bourguignon." Inspired by the renowned menu at The French Laundry, this dish is a celebration of rich textures and sophisticated taste. The succulent Brandt beef short ribs, braised to perfection, are enveloped in a velvety red wine reduction, creating a dish that pays homage to classic French cuisine with a modern twist.

Serving: 4 servings
Preparation Time: 20 minutes
Ready Time: 3 hours (including cooking time)

Ingredients:
- 4 pounds Brandt beef short ribs
- Salt and freshly ground black pepper, to taste
- 2 tablespoons vegetable oil
- 1 large onion, finely chopped
- 2 carrots, peeled and diced
- 3 cloves garlic, minced
- 1 bottle (750ml) red wine (Burgundy or Cabernet Sauvignon)
- 2 cups beef broth
- 2 tablespoons tomato paste
- 1 bouquet garni (thyme, bay leaves, parsley tied together)
- 8 ounces pearl onions, peeled
- 8 ounces cremini mushrooms, halved
- 2 tablespoons unsalted butter
- Fresh parsley, chopped (for garnish)

Instructions:
1. Preheat the Oven:
Preheat your oven to 325°F (163°C).
2. Season and Sear the Short Ribs:
Season the short ribs with salt and pepper. In a large oven-safe pot, heat the vegetable oil over medium-high heat. Sear the short ribs on all sides until golden brown. Remove and set aside.
3. Saute Aromatics:
In the same pot, add the chopped onion, carrots, and garlic. Saute until the vegetables are softened and aromatic.
4. Deglaze with Red Wine:
Pour in the red wine to deglaze the pot, scraping up any browned bits. Allow the wine to simmer and reduce by half.
5. Braise the Short Ribs:
Return the seared short ribs to the pot. Add beef broth, tomato paste, and the bouquet garni. Cover the pot and transfer it to the preheated oven. Braise for about 2.5 to 3 hours, or until the short ribs are fork-tender.
6. Prepare Mushrooms and Pearl Onions:

In a separate pan, saute the pearl onions and mushrooms in butter until golden brown and cooked through.

7. Finish the Dish:

Once the short ribs are done, remove them from the pot. Strain the braising liquid and discard the solids. Skim off excess fat. Return the short ribs, mushrooms, and pearl onions to the pot. Simmer on the stovetop until the sauce thickens.

8. Garnish and Serve:

Garnish with chopped fresh parsley and serve the Brandt Beef Short Rib Bourguignon over mashed potatoes, polenta, or a bed of buttered noodles.

Nutrition Information:

(Note: Nutritional values are approximate and may vary based on specific ingredients and portion sizes.)

- Calories: 600 per serving
- Protein: 45g
- Fat: 40g
- Carbohydrates: 8g
- Fiber: 2g
- Sugar: 3g
- Sodium: 800mg

Indulge in this luxurious Brandt Beef Short Rib Bourguignon, a dish that embodies the essence of fine dining at The French Laundry. Bon appétit!

34. Lobster "Bouillabaisse"

Indulge in the exquisite flavors of the sea with this luxurious Lobster Bouillabaisse, inspired by the culinary artistry of Thomas Keller's iconic restaurant, The French Laundry. This dish pays homage to the restaurant's commitment to perfection, bringing together the finest ingredients and meticulous preparation for a dining experience that is both sophisticated and comforting. Elevate your home kitchen to the level of a Michelin-starred establishment with this sumptuous seafood delight.

Serving: 4 servings
Preparation Time: 30 minutes

Ready Time: 1 hour 30 minutes

Ingredients:
- 2 live lobsters (about 1 1/2 pounds each)
- 1/4 cup olive oil
- 1 onion, finely chopped
- 2 leeks, white and light green parts only, thinly sliced
- 3 cloves garlic, minced
- 1 fennel bulb, thinly sliced
- 1 tablespoon tomato paste
- 1 cup dry white wine
- 1 can (28 ounces) crushed tomatoes
- 4 cups fish stock
- 1 teaspoon saffron threads
- 1 teaspoon orange zest
- 1 bay leaf
- 1 teaspoon dried thyme
- Salt and pepper, to taste
- 1/2 cup Pernod (an anise-flavored liqueur)
- 1/2 cup heavy cream
- 1/4 cup chopped fresh parsley, for garnish
- Crusty French bread, for serving

Instructions:
1. Prepare the Lobsters:
- Bring a large pot of salted water to a boil.
- Plunge the lobsters headfirst into the boiling water and cook for about 8-10 minutes until they turn bright red.
- Remove the lobsters from the water and let them cool slightly. Once cooled, crack the shells and remove the lobster meat. Cut the meat into bite-sized pieces.
2. Make the Bouillabaisse Base:
- In a large, heavy-bottomed pot, heat the olive oil over medium heat.
- Add the chopped onion, leeks, garlic, and fennel. Cook until the vegetables are softened, about 5-7 minutes.
- Stir in the tomato paste and cook for an additional 2 minutes.
- Pour in the white wine and simmer until it reduces by half.
- Add the crushed tomatoes, fish stock, saffron, orange zest, bay leaf, thyme, salt, and pepper. Bring the mixture to a simmer and cook for 30 minutes.

3. Finish the Bouillabaisse:
- Add the lobster meat to the pot and simmer for an additional 10 minutes.
- Stir in the Pernod and heavy cream. Cook for an additional 5 minutes, allowing the flavors to meld.
- Adjust the seasoning with salt and pepper to taste.
4. Serve:
- Ladle the Lobster Bouillabaisse into bowls.
- Garnish with chopped fresh parsley.
- Serve with crusty French bread on the side for a truly authentic experience.

Nutrition Information:
(Per Serving)
- Calories: 480
- Protein: 35g
- Carbohydrates: 20g
- Fat: 25g
- Saturated Fat: 8g
- Cholesterol: 200mg
- Sodium: 1200mg
- Fiber: 4g

Elevate your dining experience with this Lobster Bouillabaisse, a culinary masterpiece that captures the essence of Thomas Keller's culinary excellence at The French Laundry.

35. Red Wine-Braised Beef Cheeks

Indulge your palate in the exquisite flavors of Thomas Keller's culinary masterpiece, The French Laundry, with our Red Wine-Braised Beef Cheeks recipe. Inspired by the restaurant's dedication to perfection and bold gastronomic experiences, this dish transforms humble beef cheeks into a symphony of rich, savory, and wine-infused delight. Elevate your home cooking with this sophisticated yet comforting recipe that captures the essence of fine dining.

Serving: 4 servings
Preparation Time: 30 minutes

Ready Time: 4 hours (including braising time)

Ingredients:
- 4 beef cheeks, trimmed
- Salt and black pepper, to taste
- 2 tablespoons olive oil
- 1 onion, finely chopped
- 2 carrots, peeled and diced
- 3 garlic cloves, minced
- 2 cups red wine (choose a bold variety)
- 1 cup beef broth
- 2 tablespoons tomato paste
- 2 sprigs fresh thyme
- 2 bay leaves
- 1 tablespoon butter (optional, for finishing)

Instructions:
1. Preheat the oven to 325°F (163°C).
2. Season the beef cheeks generously with salt and black pepper.
3. In a large ovenproof Dutch oven, heat the olive oil over medium-high heat. Sear the beef cheeks until browned on all sides. Remove them from the pot and set aside.
4. In the same pot, add chopped onions and carrots. Sauté until they are softened and lightly browned. Add minced garlic and cook for an additional minute.
5. Pour in the red wine, scraping the bottom of the pot to release any flavorful bits. Stir in the beef broth and tomato paste.
6. Return the seared beef cheeks to the pot. Add fresh thyme and bay leaves. Bring the liquid to a simmer.
7. Cover the Dutch oven and transfer it to the preheated oven. Braise for approximately 3 to 3.5 hours or until the beef cheeks are fork-tender.
8. Optional: Just before serving, stir in a tablespoon of butter to add a luxurious finish to the sauce.
9. Remove the thyme sprigs and bay leaves. Adjust seasoning to taste.
10. Serve the Red Wine-Braised Beef Cheeks over mashed potatoes, polenta, or a bed of creamy risotto. Drizzle the rich red wine sauce over the top.

Nutrition Information:

Note: Nutrition information is approximate and may vary based on specific ingredients used and portion sizes.
- Calories: 450 per serving
- Protein: 30g
- Fat: 20g
- Carbohydrates: 15g
- Fiber: 3g
- Sugar: 5g
- Sodium: 700mg

Immerse yourself in the culinary brilliance of The French Laundry with this Red Wine-Braised Beef Cheeks recipe, a tribute to the timeless elegance of Thomas Keller's renowned establishment.

36. "Pastrami" of Liberty Farm Duck

Delve into the flavors of sophistication and culinary finesse with this indulgent recipe inspired by the essence of Thomas Keller's The French Laundry restaurant. The Pastrami of Liberty Farm Duck pays homage to the restaurant's dedication to quality ingredients and exquisite taste. This dish encapsulates the essence of innovation and classic flavors, marrying the rich essence of pastrami with the delectable tenderness of Liberty Farm Duck.

Serving: 4 servings
Preparation time: 30 minutes
Ready time: 5 days (including curing and resting time)

Ingredients:
- 1 whole Liberty Farm Duck breast
- 3 tablespoons kosher salt
- 2 tablespoons brown sugar
- 1 tablespoon crushed juniper berries
- 1 tablespoon whole black peppercorns
- 1 tablespoon coriander seeds
- 1 teaspoon mustard seeds
- 1 teaspoon smoked paprika
- 1 teaspoon garlic powder
- 1 bay leaf, crushed

- 1/2 teaspoon pink curing salt (optional)
- Olive oil, for searing

Instructions:
1. Prepare the Duck: Rinse the duck breast and pat dry with paper towels. Trim off any excess fat. Set aside.
2. Prepare the Cure: In a bowl, mix together kosher salt, brown sugar, crushed juniper berries, black peppercorns, coriander seeds, mustard seeds, smoked paprika, garlic powder, and crushed bay leaf. If using, add pink curing salt.
3. Cure the Duck: Place the duck breast in a shallow dish and generously coat it with the curing mixture, ensuring it is entirely covered. Cover the dish and refrigerate for 3 days, flipping the duck breast once a day to evenly distribute the cure.
4. Rinse and Dry: After 3 days, remove the duck breast from the curing mixture and rinse thoroughly under cold water. Pat dry with paper towels and allow it to air dry in the refrigerator, uncovered, for an additional 2 days. This step helps develop the pastrami's characteristic flavor and texture.
5. Sear the Duck: Preheat the oven to 300°F (150°C). In an oven-safe skillet, heat olive oil over medium-high heat. Sear the duck breast, skin side down, for 2-3 minutes until golden brown. Flip and sear the other side for an additional 2 minutes.
6. Finish in the Oven: Transfer the skillet to the preheated oven and roast the duck breast for 8-10 minutes until it reaches an internal temperature of 135°F (57°C) for medium-rare or adjust cooking time for preferred doneness. Remove from the oven and let it rest for 5 minutes before slicing.
7. Slice and Serve: Slice the pastrami-style duck breast thinly against the grain. Serve it as a standalone dish or incorporate it into sandwiches, salads, or charcuterie boards.

Nutrition Information (per serving):
Note: Nutritional values may vary based on portion sizes and ingredients used.
- Calories: Approximately 250
- Total Fat: 15g
- Saturated Fat: 4g
- Cholesterol: 95mg
- Sodium: 2100mg

- Total Carbohydrates: 4g
- Dietary Fiber: 1g
- Sugars: 2g
- Protein: 25g

Indulge in the luxurious flavors and textures of this Pastrami of Liberty Farm Duck, a dish that embodies the culinary artistry and innovation reminiscent of The French Laundry's menu.

37. Snake River Farms Pork Jowl

Indulge in the rich and succulent flavors of Snake River Farms Pork Jowl, a culinary masterpiece inspired by the renowned menu of Thomas Keller's The French Laundry. Elevate your dining experience with this exquisite dish that combines the exceptional quality of Snake River Farms pork with a luscious maple bourbon glaze, creating a harmonious symphony of taste and texture.

Serving: 4 servings
Preparation Time: 15 minutes
Ready Time: 2 hours (includes marination and cooking time)

Ingredients:
- 4 Snake River Farms Pork Jowls
- 1/2 cup pure maple syrup
- 1/4 cup bourbon
- 2 tablespoons Dijon mustard
- 2 cloves garlic, minced
- 1 teaspoon fresh thyme leaves
- Salt and black pepper to taste
- 2 tablespoons olive oil

Instructions:
1. Preheat the oven:
Preheat your oven to 325°F (163°C).
2. Prepare the glaze:
In a small saucepan, combine the maple syrup, bourbon, Dijon mustard, minced garlic, and fresh thyme leaves. Bring the mixture to a gentle

simmer over medium heat, stirring occasionally. Allow it to simmer for 5-7 minutes or until the glaze thickens slightly. Set aside.

3. Marinate the pork jowls:

Place the Snake River Farms Pork Jowls in a shallow dish. Season them with salt and black pepper, then brush each jowl generously with the prepared maple bourbon glaze. Allow the pork to marinate for at least 30 minutes, ensuring the flavors penetrate the meat.

4. Sear the pork:

Heat olive oil in an oven-safe skillet over medium-high heat. Sear the marinated pork jowls for 2-3 minutes on each side or until they develop a golden-brown crust.

5. Glaze and roast:

Brush the seared pork jowls with additional maple bourbon glaze and transfer the skillet to the preheated oven. Roast for approximately 1.5 hours, basting the jowls with the glaze every 30 minutes, until the internal temperature reaches 160°F (71°C).

6. Rest and serve:

Allow the Snake River Farms Pork Jowls to rest for 10 minutes before slicing. Serve them drizzled with any remaining glaze and garnish with fresh thyme leaves.

Nutrition Information:
- Serving Size: 1 Pork Jowl
- Calories: 420
- Total Fat: 25g
- Saturated Fat: 8g
- Cholesterol: 120mg
- Sodium: 380mg
- Total Carbohydrates: 18g
- Sugars: 15g
- Protein: 30g

Note: Nutrition information is approximate and may vary based on specific ingredients and portion sizes. Adjust accordingly based on dietary preferences and requirements.

38. Pan-Roasted Breast of Four Story Hill Farm's Poularde

Indulge in the culinary excellence inspired by Thomas Keller's iconic restaurant, The French Laundry, with our recipe for Pan-Roasted Breast of Four Story Hill Farm's Poularde. Elevate your dining experience with this exquisite dish that captures the essence of Keller's meticulous approach to gastronomy. Savor the symphony of flavors as you embark on a journey through the artistry of French cuisine.

Serving: This recipe serves 4.
Preparation Time: 30 minutes
Ready Time: 1 hour and 15 minutes

Ingredients:
- 4 Four Story Hill Farm's Poularde breasts
- 2 tablespoons olive oil
- Salt and freshly ground black pepper, to taste
- 2 tablespoons unsalted butter
- 4 sprigs fresh thyme
- 4 garlic cloves, crushed
- 1 cup chicken stock
- 1/2 cup dry white wine
- 2 tablespoons Dijon mustard
- 1 tablespoon chopped fresh parsley, for garnish

Instructions:
1. Preheat your oven to 375°F (190°C).
2. Season the Poularde breasts generously with salt and pepper on both sides.
3. In an oven-safe skillet, heat the olive oil over medium-high heat. Place the Poularde breasts in the skillet, skin side down, and sear until golden brown, approximately 4-5 minutes.
4. Flip the breasts and add the butter, thyme sprigs, and crushed garlic to the skillet. Baste the breasts with the melted butter for an additional 2-3 minutes.
5. Transfer the skillet to the preheated oven and roast for 20-25 minutes or until the internal temperature reaches 165°F (74°C).
6. Remove the skillet from the oven, transfer the breasts to a plate, and let them rest while preparing the sauce.
7. Place the skillet back on the stove over medium heat. Add chicken stock and white wine, scraping up any browned bits from the bottom of the skillet. Simmer until the liquid is reduced by half.

8. Whisk in Dijon mustard and continue to simmer until the sauce thickens slightly. Adjust the seasoning with salt and pepper to taste.
9. Spoon the sauce over the Poularde breasts, garnish with chopped parsley, and serve immediately.

Nutrition Information:
(Per serving)
- Calories: 350
- Protein: 30g
- Carbohydrates: 2g
- Fat: 23g
- Saturated Fat: 8g
- Cholesterol: 100mg
- Sodium: 400mg
- Fiber: 0g
- Sugar: 0g

Elevate your home cooking with this exquisite recipe inspired by the culinary mastery of The French Laundry. Pan-Roasted Breast of Four Story Hill Farm's Poularde is a celebration of flavors that will leave an indelible mark on your dining experience.

39. "Galette de Pommes de Terre"

The Galette de Pommes de Terre, a classic dish from Thomas Keller's iconic restaurant, The French Laundry, is an elegant yet comforting potato galette. Delicately layered potatoes are crisped to perfection, creating a dish that embodies simplicity and sophistication in each bite. This recipe pays homage to the restaurant's commitment to refined flavors and meticulous preparation, bringing a taste of its culinary finesse to your home kitchen.

Serving: Serves: 4
Preparation Time: 20 minutes
Ready Time: Cooking: 45 minutes
Total: 1 hour 5 minutes

Ingredients:
- 4 large Yukon Gold potatoes, peeled and thinly sliced

- 2 tablespoons unsalted butter, melted
- 2 tablespoons olive oil
- 2 cloves garlic, minced
- 1 teaspoon fresh thyme leaves
- Salt and pepper to taste
- Chopped fresh chives for garnish (optional)

Instructions:
1. Preheat Oven: Preheat the oven to 375°F (190°C).
2. Prepare Potatoes: Pat the potato slices dry with paper towels to remove excess moisture. In a bowl, toss the potato slices with melted butter, olive oil, minced garlic, thyme leaves, salt, and pepper, ensuring each slice is evenly coated.
3. Layer Potatoes: Arrange a layer of potato slices in a circular pattern at the bottom of a cast-iron skillet or oven-safe frying pan, slightly overlapping each slice to form a base.
4. Repeat Layers: Continue layering the potato slices in circles, building upwards until all the potato slices are used, creating a compact and layered galette.
5. Cook Galette: Place the skillet on the stovetop over medium heat for 5 minutes to lightly brown the bottom. Transfer the skillet to the preheated oven and bake for 35-40 minutes or until the potatoes are tender and the top is golden brown.
6. Serve: Once cooked, carefully remove the galette from the oven. Allow it to cool for a few minutes before gently sliding it onto a serving plate. Garnish with chopped fresh chives if desired.

Nutrition Information (per serving):
- Calories: 250
- Fat: 10g
- Carbohydrates: 35g
- Protein: 4g
- Fiber: 4g
- Sugar: 2g
- Sodium: 60mg

Note: Nutritional values are approximate and may vary based on ingredients used.

Enjoy this Galette de Pommes de Terre as a delightful side dish that pairs wonderfully with a variety of main courses or as a standalone treat, showcasing the essence of The French Laundry's culinary excellence in your own home.

40. Sweet Butter-Poached Maine Lobster Medallions

Indulge in the culinary excellence inspired by the legendary menu of Thomas Keller's The French Laundry with these delectable Sweet Butter-Poached Maine Lobster Medallions. Elevate your dining experience with the exquisite flavors and meticulous preparation that define the essence of Keller's renowned restaurant.

Serving: 4 servings
Preparation Time: 30 minutes
Ready Time: 1 hour

Ingredients:
- 4 Maine lobster tails, shell-on
- 1 cup unsalted butter, cubed
- 1/4 cup granulated sugar
- 1 vanilla bean, split and scraped
- 1 tablespoon brandy
- Zest of 1 lemon
- Salt and white pepper to taste
- Fresh chervil for garnish

Instructions:
1. Prepare the Lobster:
- Using kitchen shears, carefully cut through the top shell of each lobster tail.
- Gently pull the lobster meat from the shell, keeping it attached at the base of the tail.
2. Poaching Liquid:
- In a medium-sized saucepan over low heat, combine the butter, sugar, vanilla bean and seeds, brandy, and lemon zest.
- Stir until the sugar is dissolved, and the mixture is well combined.
3. Poaching the Lobster:
- Season the lobster medallions with salt and white pepper.

- Place the lobster meat in the poaching liquid, ensuring each medallion is fully submerged.
- Poach for 5-7 minutes, or until the lobster is opaque and cooked through. Be cautious not to overcook, as lobster can become tough.

4. Butter Basting:
- Spoon the warm butter over the lobster medallions during the poaching process for a luxurious, glossy finish.

5. Serve:
- Carefully remove the lobster from the poaching liquid and arrange on serving plates.
- Drizzle with a little of the poaching liquid and garnish with fresh chervil.

Nutrition Information:
- *(Note: Nutrition information is approximate and may vary based on specific ingredients and portion sizes.)*
- Calories: 350 per serving
- Protein: 20g
- Carbohydrates: 10g
- Fat: 25g
- Fiber: 1g
- Sugar: 9g
- Sodium: 600mg

Indulge in the extraordinary flavors of Sweet Butter-Poached Maine Lobster Medallions, a dish that pays homage to the culinary genius of Thomas Keller's iconic restaurant, The French Laundry. This exquisite recipe promises a dining experience that transcends the ordinary, making any occasion a truly special one.

41. "Poulet Rôti"

Poulet Rôti, a classic French dish, exemplifies the artistry of simple yet exquisite cuisine. Inspired by Thomas Keller's dedication to culinary perfection at The French Laundry, this roasted chicken recipe captures the essence of traditional French cooking, combining simplicity with depth of flavor. The marriage of herbs, butter, and a perfectly roasted bird creates an unforgettable dining experience, reminiscent of the timeless elegance found in fine French kitchens.

Serving: Serves: 4
Preparation Time: Preparation: 20 minutes
Ready Time: Ready in: 1 hour 30 minutes

Ingredients:
- 1 whole chicken (about 3-4 pounds)
- 4 tablespoons unsalted butter, softened
- 2 cloves garlic, minced
- 1 lemon, quartered
- 1 bunch fresh thyme
- 1 bunch fresh rosemary
- Salt and freshly ground black pepper
- Olive oil

Instructions:
1. Preheat your oven to 425°F (220°C).
2. Rinse the chicken inside and out with cold water and pat dry thoroughly with paper towels.
3. Season the cavity of the chicken generously with salt and pepper.
4. Stuff the cavity with the quartered lemon, a few sprigs of thyme, and rosemary.
5. In a small bowl, mix the softened butter with minced garlic and a pinch of salt until well combined.
6. Gently loosen the skin of the chicken by running your fingers under it, being careful not to tear it.
7. Spread the garlic herb butter under the skin, covering as much of the breast and thigh meat as possible.
8. Truss the chicken by tying the legs together with kitchen twine and tucking the wingtips under the body.
9. Place the chicken in a roasting pan and drizzle with olive oil. Season the outside generously with salt and pepper.
10. Add a few more sprigs of thyme and rosemary to the pan.
11. Roast the chicken in the preheated oven for about 1 hour and 15 minutes or until the internal temperature reaches 165°F (74°C) and the skin is golden brown and crispy.
12. Remove the chicken from the oven and let it rest for 10-15 minutes before carving.
13. Carve the chicken and serve with your choice of sides, such as roasted vegetables or a simple green salad.

Nutrition Information:
Note: Nutritional values may vary based on the size of the chicken and specific ingredients used.
- Calories: Approximately 300 calories per serving
- Fat: 18g
- Protein: 30g
- Carbohydrates: 1g
- Fiber: 0g
- Sugar: 0g
- Sodium: Varies based on added salt

42. Marcho Farms Veal Sweetbreads

Elevate your culinary experience with this exquisite dish inspired by the legendary Thomas Keller's The French Laundry restaurant. Marcho Farms Veal Sweetbreads, a delicacy celebrated for its tender texture and rich flavor, takes center stage in this exceptional recipe. Elevate your dining experience with this sophisticated dish that captures the essence of fine dining.

Serving: 4 servings
Preparation Time: 30 minutes
Ready Time: 2 hours

Ingredients:
- 1 pound Marcho Farms Veal Sweetbreads, soaked in milk for 24 hours
- 2 cups chicken stock
- 1 cup all-purpose flour
- 1 cup buttermilk
- 1 cup panko breadcrumbs
- Salt and pepper to taste
- 1/2 cup clarified butter
- 1 lemon, cut into wedges for serving
- Fresh herbs for garnish (parsley, chives)

Instructions:
1. Prepare the Sweetbreads:

- After soaking the veal sweetbreads in milk for 24 hours, drain and pat them dry with paper towels.
- Trim any excess fat and membranes from the sweetbreads.

2. Blanch the Sweetbreads:
- In a large pot, bring water to a boil.
- Blanch the sweetbreads in boiling water for 2-3 minutes.
- Immediately transfer them to an ice bath to cool.

3. Coat with Flour, Buttermilk, and Breadcrumbs:
- Set up a breading station with three shallow dishes: one with flour, one with buttermilk, and one with a mixture of panko breadcrumbs, salt, and pepper.
- Dredge each sweetbread in flour, dip into the buttermilk, and coat with the breadcrumb mixture.

4. Pan-Fry the Sweetbreads:
- Heat clarified butter in a large skillet over medium-high heat.
- Pan-fry the sweetbreads until golden brown and crispy on all sides, approximately 4-5 minutes per side.

5. Rest and Slice:
- Allow the sweetbreads to rest for a few minutes before slicing them into bite-sized pieces.

6. Prepare Chicken Stock Sauce:
- In a separate saucepan, heat chicken stock until simmering.
- Drizzle a spoonful of the hot stock over the sliced sweetbreads just before serving.

7. Garnish and Serve:
- Arrange the sweetbreads on a serving platter.
- Garnish with fresh herbs and lemon wedges.
- Serve immediately, allowing the crispy exterior and succulent interior to delight your senses.

Nutrition Information:
(Note: Nutritional values are approximate and may vary based on specific ingredients and portion sizes.)
- Calories per serving: 350
- Protein: 20g
- Fat: 18g
- Carbohydrates: 25g
- Fiber: 2g
- Sugar: 3g
- Sodium: 600mg

Immerse yourself in the culinary finesse of Thomas Keller's The French Laundry with this Marcho Farms Veal Sweetbreads recipe, where each bite is a symphony of textures and flavors.

43. Sweet Butter-Poached Maine Lobster Knuckle Sandwich

Indulge your senses in a culinary symphony inspired by the renowned Thomas Keller's The French Laundry. This Sweet Butter-Poached Maine Lobster Knuckle Sandwich takes the essence of fine dining and transforms it into a delightful handheld masterpiece. The succulent sweetness of Maine lobster, gently poached in luscious butter, is harmoniously paired with a medley of flavors, creating a sandwich that transcends the ordinary.

Serving: Serves 4
Preparation Time: 20 minutes
Ready Time: 30 minutes

Ingredients:
- 1 pound Maine lobster knuckle meat, cooked and chopped
- 1/2 cup unsalted butter
- 2 tablespoons honey
- 1 tablespoon Dijon mustard
- 1 teaspoon fresh lemon juice
- 1/4 teaspoon sea salt
- 1/4 teaspoon black pepper
- 1/4 cup finely chopped chives
- 8 slices brioche bread
- 4 butter lettuce leaves

Instructions:
1. Prepare the Lobster:
- If not already cooked, steam or boil the lobster until the knuckle meat is tender. Remove the meat from the shell and chop it into bite-sized pieces.
2. Poach the Lobster:

- In a medium-sized skillet over low heat, melt the unsalted butter. Add honey, Dijon mustard, fresh lemon juice, sea salt, and black pepper. Stir until well combined.
- Gently place the chopped lobster knuckle meat into the skillet, ensuring each piece is coated in the sweet butter mixture. Poach for 5-7 minutes, allowing the flavors to meld and the lobster to absorb the decadent essence.

3. Assemble the Sandwich:
- Toast the brioche slices until golden brown. Place a butter lettuce leaf on four of the slices.
- Spoon the butter-poached lobster knuckle meat onto the lettuce, distributing it evenly among the four slices.

4. Garnish and Close the Sandwich:
- Sprinkle finely chopped chives over the lobster. Top each sandwich with the remaining four slices of toasted brioche.

5. Serve:
- Arrange the Sweet Butter-Poached Maine Lobster Knuckle Sandwiches on a platter. Optionally, cut them in half for easier handling.

Nutrition Information:
(Per serving)
- Calories: 520
- Total Fat: 34g
- Saturated Fat: 20g
- Trans Fat: 0g
- Cholesterol: 150mg
- Sodium: 680mg
- Total Carbohydrates: 31g
- Dietary Fiber: 1g
- Sugars: 9g
- Protein: 23g

Elevate your dining experience with this exquisite Sweet Butter-Poached Maine Lobster Knuckle Sandwich, a culinary homage to the innovation and artistry of Thomas Keller's iconic creations at The French Laundry.

44. Roasted Rack of Elysian Fields Farm Lamb

Elevate your dining experience with this exquisite recipe inspired by the renowned Thomas Keller's The French Laundry restaurant. The Roasted Rack of Elysian Fields Farm Lamb is a culinary masterpiece that captures the essence of fine dining. The succulent flavors of perfectly roasted lamb, combined with carefully selected herbs and spices, create a dish that is sure to leave a lasting impression on your guests.

Serving: 4 servings
Preparation Time: 20 minutes
Ready Time: 1 hour 30 minutes

Ingredients:
- 2 racks of Elysian Fields Farm lamb (about 1 1/2 pounds each), frenched
- Salt and black pepper, to taste
- 2 tablespoons Dijon mustard
- 2 tablespoons olive oil
- 3 cloves garlic, minced
- 1 tablespoon fresh rosemary, finely chopped
- 1 tablespoon fresh thyme leaves
- 1 teaspoon dried oregano
- 1 teaspoon paprika

Instructions:
1. Preheat your oven to 375°F (190°C).
2. Season the racks of lamb with salt and black pepper, ensuring an even coating on all sides.
3. In a small bowl, mix together the Dijon mustard, olive oil, minced garlic, rosemary, thyme, oregano, and paprika to create a flavorful herb rub.
4. Coat the racks of lamb with the herb rub, massaging it into the meat for maximum flavor.
5. Heat a large oven-safe skillet over medium-high heat. Sear the lamb racks on all sides until golden brown, approximately 2-3 minutes per side.
6. Transfer the skillet to the preheated oven and roast the lamb for about 25-30 minutes for medium-rare, or until the internal temperature reaches 130°F (54°C). Adjust the time for your preferred level of doneness.

7. Remove the lamb from the oven and let it rest for 10 minutes before carving. This allows the juices to redistribute and ensures a juicy, tender result.
8. Slice the racks into individual chops and arrange them on a serving platter.
9. Optionally, drizzle with a bit of extra olive oil and sprinkle with fresh herbs for a finishing touch.

Nutrition Information:
(Per Serving)
- Calories: 450
- Protein: 30g
- Total Fat: 36g
- Saturated Fat: 12g
- Cholesterol: 100mg
- Sodium: 300mg
- Total Carbohydrates: 1g
- Dietary Fiber: 0g
- Sugars: 0g

Indulge in the divine flavors of this Roasted Rack of Elysian Fields Farm Lamb, a dish that mirrors the culinary excellence of Thomas Keller's iconic restaurant.

45. "Ballotine" of Liberty Farms Pekin Duck Foie Gras

Indulge in the culinary artistry inspired by Thomas Keller's iconic restaurant, The French Laundry, with this exquisite recipe for "Ballotine of Liberty Farms Pekin Duck Foie Gras." Elevate your dining experience with the harmonious blend of premium ingredients and expert techniques, reflecting the culinary excellence synonymous with Keller's gastronomic legacy.

Serving: Serves 4
Preparation Time: 30 minutes
Ready Time: 24 hours (including chilling time)

Ingredients:

- 1 whole Liberty Farms Pekin Duck Foie Gras (about 1.5 pounds)
- 1 teaspoon kosher salt
- 1/2 teaspoon freshly ground black pepper
- 1/4 teaspoon curing salt (optional)
- 1/4 cup Sauternes wine
- 1 tablespoon truffle oil
- 4 slices prosciutto
- 2 tablespoons finely chopped fresh chives
- 1 tablespoon finely chopped fresh parsley
- 1 tablespoon cognac

Instructions:
1. Prepare the Foie Gras:
- Carefully devein the foie gras, removing any visible veins. Use a sharp knife to separate the lobes.
- Season the foie gras with kosher salt, black pepper, and curing salt (if using). Drizzle Sauternes wine over the foie gras.
2. Marinate:
- Allow the foie gras to marinate in the wine for at least 20 minutes, ensuring the flavors penetrate the delicate texture.
3. Sear the Foie Gras:
- In a hot pan, sear the foie gras for about 30 seconds on each side until golden brown. Remove from heat and let it cool slightly.
4. Assemble the Ballotine:
- Lay out the prosciutto slices slightly overlapping. Place the seared foie gras on top. Sprinkle chives and parsley over the foie gras.
- Carefully roll the foie gras in the prosciutto to form a tight log. Secure with kitchen twine.
5. Chill:
- Wrap the foie gras tightly in plastic wrap and refrigerate for at least 24 hours. This allows the flavors to meld and the ballotine to set.
6. Serve:
- Before serving, remove the ballotine from the refrigerator and let it come to room temperature. Drizzle with truffle oil and cognac.
7. Slice and Enjoy:
- Slice the ballotine into rounds and serve on toasted brioche or a bed of mixed greens. Garnish with additional chives and a drizzle of truffle oil.

Nutrition Information:
(Per serving - based on a serving size of one-fourth of the recipe)

- Calories: XXX
- Protein: XXX g
- Fat: XXX g
- Carbohydrates: XXX g
- Fiber: XXX g
- Sugar: XXX g
- Sodium: XXX mg

Delight in the rich, luxurious flavors of this Ballotine of Liberty Farms Pekin Duck Foie Gras, a culinary masterpiece inspired by the esteemed Thomas Keller and his iconic French Laundry restaurant.

46. Broiled Japanese Bluefin Tuna

Elevate your culinary experience with the exquisite flavors of Broiled Japanese Bluefin Tuna, a dish inspired by the renowned menu of Thomas Keller's The French Laundry restaurant. This recipe combines the finest quality tuna with Japanese culinary techniques to create a masterpiece that tantalizes the taste buds. The simplicity of the preparation allows the natural richness of the tuna to shine, making it a perfect choice for those seeking a sophisticated and flavorful dining experience.

Serving: 4 servings
Preparation Time: 15 minutes
Ready Time: 25 minutes

Ingredients:
- 4 Japanese Bluefin Tuna steaks (about 6 ounces each)
- 2 tablespoons soy sauce
- 1 tablespoon mirin (Japanese sweet rice wine)
- 1 tablespoon sake
- 1 tablespoon sesame oil
- 1 teaspoon grated fresh ginger
- 2 cloves garlic, minced
- 1 tablespoon honey
- 1 tablespoon chopped green onions (for garnish)
- Sesame seeds (for garnish)
- Lemon wedges (for serving)

Instructions:
1. Preheat the Broiler:
- Adjust the oven rack to the top position and preheat the broiler.
2. Prepare the Marinade:
- In a small bowl, whisk together soy sauce, mirin, sake, sesame oil, grated ginger, minced garlic, and honey.
3. Marinate the Tuna:
- Place the tuna steaks in a shallow dish and pour half of the marinade over them. Ensure the tuna is well-coated. Let it marinate for 10 minutes.
4. Broil the Tuna:
- Transfer the marinated tuna steaks to a broiler-safe pan. Broil for 3-4 minutes per side, or until the edges are seared, and the center is still slightly pink.
5. Baste with Marinade:
- While broiling, baste the tuna with the remaining marinade to enhance the flavor and moisture.
6. Garnish and Serve:
- Once the tuna is cooked to your liking, remove it from the broiler. Sprinkle chopped green onions and sesame seeds over the top for garnish. Serve hot with lemon wedges on the side.

Nutrition Information:
(Per Serving)
- Calories: 300
- Protein: 30g
- Carbohydrates: 8g
- Fat: 15g
- Saturated Fat: 2g
- Cholesterol: 45mg
- Sodium: 600mg
- Fiber: 1g
- Sugar: 6g

Note: Nutrition information is approximate and may vary based on specific ingredients used.

47. Sauteed Fillet of Mediterranean Loup de Mer

Elevate your culinary skills with this exquisite recipe inspired by the renowned Thomas Keller's The French Laundry restaurant. Our Sauteed Fillet of Mediterranean Loup de Mer pays homage to the restaurant's commitment to precision and quality. The dish showcases the delicate flavors of the Mediterranean sea bass, harmoniously brought together through a masterful sautéing technique. Immerse yourself in the art of fine dining with this delectable creation.

Serving: 4 servings
Preparation Time: 20 minutes
Ready Time: 30 minutes

Ingredients:
- 4 fillets of Mediterranean Loup de Mer (Sea Bass), skin on
- 2 tablespoons olive oil
- Salt and pepper, to taste
- 1 lemon, thinly sliced
- 2 tablespoons unsalted butter
- 2 cloves garlic, minced
- 1 tablespoon fresh parsley, chopped
- 1 teaspoon capers, drained

Instructions:
1. Prepare the Loup de Mer:
- Pat the fillets dry with paper towels to remove excess moisture.
- Season both sides of the fillets with salt and pepper.
2. Sauté the Fillets:
- In a large, oven-safe skillet, heat olive oil over medium-high heat.
- Place the fillets in the skillet, skin side down, and cook for 3-4 minutes or until the skin is crispy and golden brown.
- Carefully flip the fillets and cook the other side for an additional 2-3 minutes.
- Add lemon slices to the skillet, allowing them to caramelize alongside the fish.
3. Finish in the Oven:
- Preheat the oven broiler.
- Transfer the skillet to the oven and broil for 2-3 minutes or until the fish is cooked through and flakes easily with a fork.
4. Prepare the Sauce:
- In a small saucepan, melt butter over medium heat.

- Add minced garlic and cook for 1-2 minutes until fragrant.
- Stir in chopped parsley and capers. Cook for an additional 1-2 minutes.
5. Serve:
- Plate the sautéed fillets, drizzling the garlic-caper sauce over the top.
- Garnish with additional fresh parsley and lemon slices if desired.

Nutrition Information:
(Per Serving)
- Calories: 320
- Protein: 28g
- Fat: 20g
- Carbohydrates: 5g
- Fiber: 1g
- Sugars: 1g
- Sodium: 400mg

Indulge in the sophistication of The French Laundry with this Sauteed Fillet of Mediterranean Loup de Mer—a dish that marries simplicity with sublime flavors.

48. Snake River Farms Pork Belly Confit

Indulge your taste buds in the exquisite flavors reminiscent of Thomas Keller's iconic dishes at The French Laundry with this Snake River Farms Pork Belly Confit recipe. A masterpiece of culinary finesse, this dish pays homage to the restaurant's commitment to exceptional ingredients and meticulous preparation. Elevate your dining experience with the succulent and rich flavors of Snake River Farms Pork Belly, expertly slow-cooked to perfection. Delight in the symphony of textures and aromas that make this dish a standout in the world of gourmet cuisine.

Serving: 4 servings
Preparation Time: 15 minutes
Ready Time: 8 hours (including marination and cooking time)

Ingredients:
- 2 lbs Snake River Farms Pork Belly, skin-on
- 1/4 cup kosher salt

- 1/4 cup granulated sugar
- 1 tablespoon black peppercorns, crushed
- 4 cloves garlic, smashed
- 4 sprigs fresh thyme
- 2 bay leaves
- 2 cups duck fat (or a mixture of duck fat and pork fat)

Instructions:

1. Prep the Pork Belly:
- Rinse the pork belly and pat it dry with paper towels.
- In a small bowl, combine kosher salt, sugar, and crushed black peppercorns.
- Rub the salt mixture all over the pork belly, ensuring an even coating.
- Place the pork belly in a large dish and refrigerate, uncovered, for at least 4 hours or overnight to allow the salt to penetrate.

2. Marinate:
- After the initial refrigeration, remove the pork belly from the fridge.
- Rinse off the excess salt under cold water and pat it dry.
- Place the pork belly in a sealable plastic bag and add smashed garlic, fresh thyme, and bay leaves.
- Seal the bag, removing as much air as possible, and refrigerate for another 4 hours to let the flavors meld.

3. Confit Cooking:
- Preheat your oven to 225°F (107°C).
- Remove the pork belly from the refrigerator and let it come to room temperature.
- In a deep, oven-safe dish, melt the duck fat over low heat until it becomes a liquid.
- Place the marinated pork belly in the dish, ensuring it is fully submerged in the melted fat.
- Cover the dish with a lid or foil and transfer it to the preheated oven.
- Slow-cook the pork belly for about 6-8 hours or until it becomes tender and easily pierced with a fork.

4. Finish and Serve:
- Carefully remove the confit pork belly from the oven.
- Gently lift the pork belly from the fat and let it drain briefly on a paper towel.
- Heat a skillet over medium-high heat and sear the pork belly on each side until golden and crispy.

- Slice the pork belly into portions and serve hot, garnished with fresh herbs if desired.

Nutrition Information:
(Per Serving)
- Calories: 600
- Total Fat: 55g
- Saturated Fat: 20g
- Cholesterol: 90mg
- Sodium: 1200mg
- Total Carbohydrates: 5g
- Dietary Fiber: 1g
- Sugars: 3g
- Protein: 20g

Savor the extraordinary taste of The French Laundry's inspiration with this Snake River Farms Pork Belly Confit—a dish that brings together the mastery of technique and the highest quality ingredients.

49. Roasted Sirloin of Brandt Beef

Indulge your culinary senses with a spectacular dish inspired by the renowned Thomas Keller's The French Laundry restaurant. This recipe for Roasted Sirloin of Brandt Beef captures the essence of fine dining, offering a perfect blend of exquisite flavors and expertly prepared beef. Elevate your dining experience with this sophisticated creation that pays homage to the culinary excellence of The French Laundry.

Serving: 4 servings
Preparation Time: 20 minutes
Ready Time: 1 hour and 30 minutes

Ingredients:
- 2 lbs Brandt Beef sirloin
- 2 tablespoons olive oil
- 4 cloves garlic, minced
- 2 teaspoons fresh thyme leaves
- Salt and pepper to taste

For the Red Wine Reduction:

- 1 cup red wine
- 1/2 cup beef broth
- 2 tablespoons unsalted butter

Instructions:
1. Preheat the Oven:
Preheat your oven to 400°F (200°C).
2. Prepare the Beef:
- Pat the sirloin dry with paper towels to remove excess moisture.
- Rub the beef with olive oil, ensuring an even coating.
- Season with minced garlic, fresh thyme leaves, salt, and pepper, pressing the seasonings into the meat.
3. Sear the Sirloin:
- Heat a large, oven-safe skillet over medium-high heat.
- Sear the sirloin on all sides until a golden-brown crust forms, approximately 3-4 minutes per side.
4. Roast in the Oven:
- Transfer the skillet to the preheated oven.
- Roast the sirloin for about 1 hour or until the internal temperature reaches your desired level of doneness (135°F for medium-rare).
5. Make the Red Wine Reduction:
- In a saucepan, combine red wine and beef broth.
- Simmer over medium heat until the liquid reduces by half.
- Whisk in unsalted butter until the sauce thickens. Season with salt and pepper to taste.
6. Rest and Slice:
- Allow the roasted sirloin to rest for 10 minutes before slicing.
- Slice the sirloin into thin, elegant portions.
7. Serve with Red Wine Reduction:
- Plate the sliced sirloin and drizzle the red wine reduction over the top.

Nutrition Information:
- *Calories:* 400 per serving
- *Protein:* 30g
- *Carbohydrates:* 2g
- *Fat:* 28g
- *Cholesterol:* 90mg
- *Sodium:* 350mg

Indulge in the decadent flavors of this Roasted Sirloin of Brandt Beef, a masterpiece inspired by the culinary genius of Thomas Keller's The

French Laundry. This dish promises to elevate your dining experience to new heights, making every bite a celebration of exquisite taste and culinary artistry.

50. Crispy-Skinned Striped Bass

Indulge in the culinary elegance inspired by the renowned menu of Thomas Keller's iconic restaurant, The French Laundry. Our Crispy-Skinned Striped Bass pays homage to the restaurant's commitment to perfection and fine dining. This dish showcases the delicate flavors of striped bass beneath a golden, crispy skin—a testament to the artistry that defines The French Laundry experience.

Serving: 4 servings
Preparation Time: 15 minutes
Ready Time: 30 minutes

Ingredients:
- 4 striped bass fillets (6-8 ounces each), scaled and deboned
- Salt and freshly ground black pepper, to taste
- 2 tablespoons olive oil
- 1 tablespoon unsalted butter
- 4 sprigs fresh thyme
- Lemon wedges, for serving

Instructions:
1. Preheat the Oven:
Preheat your oven to 400°F (200°C).
2. Prepare the Striped Bass:
Pat the striped bass fillets dry with paper towels. Season both sides with salt and pepper.
3. Crisp the Skin:
Heat olive oil in an oven-safe skillet over medium-high heat. Place the bass fillets in the skillet, skin-side down. Allow them to cook undisturbed for about 3-4 minutes, ensuring the skin becomes golden and crispy.
4. Add Butter and Thyme:

Add butter and thyme sprigs to the skillet. Spoon the melted butter over the fish to baste it. Continue cooking for an additional 2 minutes on the stove.

5. Transfer to Oven:

Transfer the skillet to the preheated oven and bake for 8-10 minutes, or until the fish is cooked through and flakes easily with a fork.

6. Serve:

Carefully remove the skillet from the oven. Discard thyme sprigs. Serve the crispy-skinned striped bass fillets on individual plates, drizzling any remaining pan juices over the top. Accompany with lemon wedges for a burst of freshness.

Nutrition Information:
(Per Serving)
- Calories: 320
- Total Fat: 18g
- Saturated Fat: 5g
- Cholesterol: 80mg
- Sodium: 90mg
- Total Carbohydrates: 1g
- Protein: 38g

Indulge in the luxurious simplicity of Crispy-Skinned Striped Bass—a dish that captures the essence of The French Laundry's culinary excellence.

51. "Oeufs et Oignons"

Indulge in the culinary artistry inspired by Thomas Keller's iconic The French Laundry with this exquisite recipe for "Oeufs et Oignons." Translating to "Eggs and Onions," this dish showcases the delicate balance of flavors and textures that define the French culinary tradition. Elevate your dining experience and embark on a journey of gastronomic delight with this sophisticated creation.

Serving: 2 servings
Preparation Time: 15 minutes
Ready Time: 30 minutes

Ingredients:
- 4 large eggs
- 1 large onion, thinly sliced
- 2 tablespoons unsalted butter
- Salt and black pepper, to taste
- 1 tablespoon chives, finely chopped (for garnish)
- Crème fraîche (optional, for serving)

Instructions:
1. Caramelize the Onions:
- In a skillet over medium heat, melt 1 tablespoon of butter.
- Add the thinly sliced onions and sauté until they become golden brown and caramelized, stirring occasionally. This process may take about 15-20 minutes. Season with a pinch of salt and set aside.
2. Prepare the Eggs:
- In a separate non-stick pan, melt the remaining butter over medium-low heat.
- Crack the eggs into the pan, ensuring not to break the yolks.
- Cook the eggs gently, allowing the whites to set while keeping the yolks runny.
3. Assemble the Dish:
- Place a generous spoonful of caramelized onions on each plate.
- Carefully transfer the cooked eggs on top of the onions.
- Season with salt and black pepper to taste.
4. Garnish:
- Sprinkle finely chopped chives over the eggs for a burst of freshness.
5. Serve:
- Optionally, serve with a dollop of crème fraîche on the side.

Nutrition Information:
(Note: Nutrition information may vary based on specific ingredients and serving sizes. The values provided are approximate.)
- Calories: 250 per serving
- Protein: 12g
- Fat: 18g
- Carbohydrates: 8g
- Fiber: 2g
- Sugar: 4g
- Sodium: 350mg

Delight in the harmonious blend of creamy eggs and the rich sweetness of caramelized onions, a dish that encapsulates the essence of Thomas Keller's culinary mastery at The French Laundry. Enjoy the artistry of French cuisine in the comfort of your own home with this inspired recipe.

52. Pan-Seared Fillet of Gulf Coast Cobia

Inspired by the culinary excellence of Thomas Keller's The French Laundry, this recipe showcases the exquisite flavors of the Gulf Coast with a Pan-Seared Fillet of Cobia. Cobia, a versatile and delicious fish, takes center stage in this dish, marrying perfectly with a harmonious blend of flavors and textures. Elevate your dining experience with this gourmet creation that pays homage to the renowned culinary legacy of The French Laundry.

Serving: 4 servings
Preparation Time: 20 minutes
Ready Time: 30 minutes

Ingredients:
- 4 Gulf Coast Cobia fillets (6-8 ounces each)
- 2 tablespoons olive oil
- Salt and pepper to taste
- 1 tablespoon unsalted butter
For the Lemon Beurre Blanc:
- 1/2 cup dry white wine
- 1/4 cup white wine vinegar
- 2 tablespoons minced shallots
- 1 tablespoon heavy cream
- 1/2 cup cold unsalted butter, cut into cubes
- Juice of 1 lemon
- Salt and white pepper to taste
For the Herbed Quinoa:
- 1 cup quinoa, rinsed
- 2 cups chicken or vegetable broth
- 2 tablespoons chopped fresh parsley
- 1 tablespoon chopped fresh chives

- Salt and pepper to taste

Instructions:
1. Prepare the Lemon Beurre Blanc:
- In a saucepan, combine white wine, white wine vinegar, and shallots. Simmer over medium heat until the liquid is reduced by half.
- Add heavy cream and reduce heat to low. Whisk in the cold butter cubes gradually until the sauce is smooth.
- Stir in lemon juice and season with salt and white pepper. Keep warm on low heat while preparing the fish.

2. Cook the Herbed Quinoa:
- In a medium saucepan, bring the chicken or vegetable broth to a boil.
- Add quinoa, reduce heat to low, cover, and simmer for 15-20 minutes or until the liquid is absorbed and quinoa is tender.
- Fluff the quinoa with a fork and stir in chopped parsley, chives, salt, and pepper.

3. Prepare the Gulf Coast Cobia:
- Pat the Cobia fillets dry with paper towels and season with salt and pepper.
- In a large skillet, heat olive oil over medium-high heat. Place the fillets in the skillet, skin side down, and sear for 3-4 minutes until the skin is crispy.
- Flip the fillets, add butter to the skillet, and continue cooking for another 3-4 minutes until the fish is cooked through and flakes easily.

4. Assemble:
- Place a generous spoonful of herbed quinoa on each plate.
- Top with a pan-seared Cobia fillet.
- Drizzle the Lemon Beurre Blanc sauce over the fish.
- Garnish with additional fresh herbs if desired.

Nutrition Information (per serving):
- Calories: 450
- Protein: 28g
- Fat: 28g
- Carbohydrates: 20g
- Fiber: 2g
- Sugar: 1g
- Sodium: 350mg

Elevate your home cooking with the sophistication and flavors reminiscent of The French Laundry, and savor the taste of the Gulf Coast in every delightful bite.

53. Herb-Crusted Sautéed Fillet of Alaskan King Salmon

Drawing inspiration from the refined flavors of Thomas Keller's The French Laundry restaurant, this Herb-Crusted Sautéed Fillet of Alaskan King Salmon embodies sophistication and exquisite taste. The harmonious blend of herbs atop a perfectly sautéed salmon fillet delivers a culinary experience worthy of any fine dining table.

Serving: Serves: 4
Pairs well with a side of roasted vegetables or a light salad for a complete meal.
Preparation Time: Prep Time: 15 minutes
Ready Time: Total Time: 25 minutes

Ingredients:
- 4 Alaskan King Salmon fillets (6 ounces each), skin on
- 2 tablespoons olive oil
- Salt and freshly ground black pepper to taste

For the Herb Crust:
- 1 cup fresh breadcrumbs (from day-old bread)
- 2 tablespoons chopped fresh parsley
- 1 tablespoon chopped fresh dill
- 1 tablespoon chopped fresh chives
- 1 tablespoon chopped fresh tarragon
- 2 cloves garlic, minced
- Zest of 1 lemon
- 2 tablespoons unsalted butter, melted

Instructions:
1. Preheat the oven to 375°F (190°C). Line a baking sheet with parchment paper.

2. In a mixing bowl, combine the breadcrumbs, chopped parsley, dill, chives, tarragon, minced garlic, lemon zest, and melted butter. Mix until the herbs are evenly distributed throughout the breadcrumbs.
3. Pat the salmon fillets dry with paper towels and season both sides generously with salt and pepper.
4. Heat olive oil in an ovenproof skillet over medium-high heat. Once the oil is hot, place the salmon fillets in the skillet, skin side down. Sear for 2-3 minutes until the skin is crispy and golden brown.
5. Remove the skillet from the heat. Spread the herb crust mixture evenly over the top of each salmon fillet, pressing gently to adhere.
6. Transfer the skillet to the preheated oven and bake for 8-10 minutes, or until the salmon is cooked through and the crust is golden brown and crisp.
7. Carefully remove the skillet from the oven. Using a spatula, transfer the salmon fillets to serving plates.
8. Serve the Herb-Crusted Sautéed Fillet of Alaskan King Salmon immediately, garnished with additional fresh herbs if desired.

Nutrition Information (per serving):
Calories: 380kcal
Protein: 34g
Fat: 24g
Saturated Fat: 6g
Cholesterol: 100mg
Sodium: 410mg
Carbohydrates: 6g
Fiber: 1g
Sugar: 1g

54. Pan-Roasted Maine Lobster Tail

The Pan-Roasted Maine Lobster Tail is a sumptuous dish inspired by the culinary excellence of Thomas Keller's The French Laundry restaurant. This recipe beautifully marries the exquisite flavors of Maine lobster with a simple yet elegant pan-roasting technique, resulting in a dish that embodies sophistication and taste.

Serving: This recipe serves 2 people, making it a perfect indulgence for an intimate dinner or a special occasion.
Preparation Time: 15 minutes
Ready Time: 30 minutes

Ingredients:
- 2 Maine lobster tails, thawed if frozen
- 2 tablespoons unsalted butter
- 2 cloves garlic, minced
- 1 tablespoon fresh parsley, finely chopped
- Salt and black pepper to taste
- Lemon wedges for serving

Instructions:
1. Preheat your oven to 400°F (200°C).
2. Prepare the lobster tails by using kitchen shears to cut through the top shell lengthwise, stopping at the tail. Gently pry the shell open, keeping the meat attached at the base. Carefully lift the meat through the slit you created in the shell, resting it on top. Season the exposed lobster meat with salt and black pepper.
3. In an oven-safe skillet, melt the butter over medium-high heat. Add minced garlic and cook for about 30 seconds until fragrant but not browned.
4. Place the seasoned lobster tails in the skillet, shell side down. Sear for 2-3 minutes until the shells start to turn red and slightly caramelized.
5. Transfer the skillet to the preheated oven and roast the lobster tails for 8-10 minutes until the meat is opaque and cooked through. Baste the lobster tails with the melted butter occasionally during roasting.
6. Once done, remove the skillet from the oven. Sprinkle the lobster tails with chopped parsley for added freshness and flavor.
7. Serve the Pan-Roasted Maine Lobster Tails immediately, accompanied by lemon wedges for a citrusy touch.

Nutrition Information (per serving):
- Calories: Approximately 200 kcal
- Protein: 20g
- Fat: 10g
- Carbohydrates: 2g
- Fiber: 0g
- Sugars: 0g

- Sodium: Varies based on added salt
Note: Nutritional values may vary based on specific ingredients used and can be adjusted based on individual dietary needs or preferences.

55. Seared Brandt Beef Tenderloin

The French Laundry, a bastion of culinary excellence, inspires this sumptuous dish showcasing the exquisite Seared Brandt Beef Tenderloin. Elevating the classic beef tenderloin to new heights, this recipe embodies the restaurant's dedication to premium ingredients and meticulous preparation. With a perfect sear that locks in juices, the tenderness of Brandt beef shines through in every decadent bite.

Serving: Serves: 4
Serving Size: 1 beef tenderloin
Preparation Time: 15 minutes
Marination: 2 hours (optional)
Ready Time: Total: Approximately 2 hours 30 minutes (including marination time)

Ingredients:
- 4 pieces Brandt Beef Tenderloin (6-8 ounces each), trimmed
- 2 tablespoons olive oil
- 2 cloves garlic, minced
- 2 sprigs fresh thyme
- Salt and freshly ground black pepper, to taste
- 2 tablespoons unsalted butter
- 2 sprigs rosemary

Instructions:
1. Preparation: Remove the beef tenderloin from the refrigerator at least 30 minutes before cooking to bring it to room temperature. Pat the beef dry with paper towels and season generously with salt and pepper on all sides.
2. Optional Marination (for added flavor): Combine olive oil, minced garlic, and thyme in a shallow dish. Place the seasoned beef tenderloins in the marinade, cover, and refrigerate for at least 2 hours or overnight.

3. Searing the Beef: Heat a heavy-bottomed skillet over high heat. Add olive oil to the skillet and let it heat until shimmering. Carefully place the beef tenderloins in the skillet, ensuring they're not crowded, and sear for 3-4 minutes on each side until a deep golden crust forms. Add the butter and rosemary to the skillet, continuously basting the beef with the melted butter for added flavor.

4. Resting and Serving: Remove the seared beef tenderloins from the skillet and let them rest on a cutting board for 5-7 minutes to allow the juices to redistribute. Slice the tenderloins against the grain into medallions and arrange them on serving plates. Garnish with additional fresh herbs if desired.

Nutrition Information (per serving)
- Calories: 350
- Total Fat: 24g
- Saturated Fat: 9g
- Cholesterol: 100mg
- Sodium: 110mg
- Protein: 30g
- Iron: 3mg
- Potassium: 520mg
- Total Carbohydrates: 0g
- Dietary Fiber: 0g
- Sugars: 0g

This dish of Seared Brandt Beef Tenderloin embodies the finesse and elegance characteristic of The French Laundry's cuisine. Each bite encapsulates the rich flavors and impeccable technique that define this renowned establishment's culinary prowess.

56. Grilled Japanese Wagyu Ribeye

Indulge in the epitome of culinary luxury with our Grilled Japanese Wagyu Ribeye, a dish inspired by the exquisite menu of Thomas Keller's iconic restaurant, The French Laundry. Elevate your dining experience with the rich marbling and unparalleled tenderness of Japanese Wagyu, perfectly grilled to perfection. This recipe is a celebration of exceptional ingredients and meticulous preparation, reminiscent of the world-class standards set by The French Laundry.

Serving: 4 servings
Preparation Time: 20 minutes
Ready Time: 30 minutes

Ingredients:
- 4 Japanese Wagyu Ribeye steaks (approximately 8 ounces each)
- 2 tablespoons high-quality olive oil
- 2 teaspoons sea salt
- 1 teaspoon freshly ground black pepper
- 4 sprigs of fresh thyme

Instructions:
1. Preheat the Grill:
Preheat your grill to high heat. For an added layer of flavor, you can use a charcoal grill with hardwood charcoal.
2. Prepare the Wagyu Ribeye:
Remove the Japanese Wagyu Ribeye steaks from the refrigerator and let them come to room temperature for about 15 minutes. This ensures even cooking.
3. Season the Steaks:
Brush each side of the steaks with olive oil, ensuring they are well-coated. Sprinkle sea salt and freshly ground black pepper generously on both sides. Gently press the seasoning into the meat.
4. Grilling:
Place the Wagyu Ribeye steaks on the preheated grill. For a perfect medium-rare doneness, grill for approximately 3-4 minutes per side. Adjust the cooking time according to your desired level of doneness.
5. Thyme Infusion:
In the last minute of grilling, place a sprig of fresh thyme on each steak, allowing the heat to release its aromatic oils and infuse the meat with an additional layer of flavor.
6. Resting:
Once the steaks are grilled to perfection, remove them from the grill and let them rest for about 5 minutes. This allows the juices to redistribute, ensuring a moist and flavorful result.
7. Serve:
Plate the Grilled Japanese Wagyu Ribeye steaks and garnish with additional fresh thyme. Pair with your favorite side dishes or a simple green salad to complement the richness of the Wagyu.

Nutrition Information:
(Per Serving)
- Calories: 600
- Protein: 32g
- Fat: 52g
- Carbohydrates: 0g
- Fiber: 0g
- Sugars: 0g

Indulge in this extraordinary dish, paying homage to the culinary brilliance of Thomas Keller's The French Laundry, and savor the unmatched quality of Grilled Japanese Wagyu Ribeye.

57. Roasted Venison Loin

Indulge your senses in the exquisite flavors of Thomas Keller's culinary masterpiece, The French Laundry, with our inspired recipe for Roasted Venison Loin. Elevate your dining experience with the rich, succulent taste of venison, expertly roasted to perfection. This dish pays homage to the meticulous attention to detail and uncompromising quality that defines Keller's renowned restaurant.

Serving: 4 servings
Preparation Time: 30 minutes
Ready Time: 1 hour 30 minutes

Ingredients:
- 2 lbs venison loin
- 2 tablespoons olive oil
- 2 tablespoons unsalted butter
- Salt and black pepper, to taste
- 2 sprigs fresh thyme
- 2 sprigs fresh rosemary
- 4 garlic cloves, minced
- 1 cup red wine
- 1 cup beef or venison broth

Instructions:

1. Preheat the Oven:
Preheat your oven to 375°F (190°C).
2. Prepare the Venison:
Pat the venison loin dry with paper towels. Season generously with salt and black pepper.
3. Sear the Venison:
In an oven-safe skillet, heat olive oil over medium-high heat. Sear the venison on all sides until golden brown. Add butter, thyme, rosemary, and minced garlic to the skillet.
4. Roast in the Oven:
Transfer the skillet to the preheated oven. Roast the venison for 15-20 minutes for medium-rare or adjust the time to your preferred doneness.
5. Rest the Venison:
Once roasted, remove the venison from the oven and let it rest on a cutting board for 10 minutes before slicing.
6. Prepare the Sauce:
Place the skillet back on the stovetop over medium heat. Deglaze the pan with red wine, scraping up any browned bits. Add the broth and simmer until the sauce thickens.
7. Slice and Serve:
Slice the venison into medallions and drizzle with the rich pan sauce. Garnish with fresh herbs if desired.

Nutrition Information:
(Note: Nutritional values are approximate and may vary based on specific ingredients and serving sizes.)
- Calories: 400 per serving
- Protein: 40g
- Fat: 20g
- Carbohydrates: 5g
- Fiber: 1g
- Sugars: 1g

Elevate your dining experience with this Roasted Venison Loin recipe, inspired by the culinary genius of Thomas Keller. Each bite is a symphony of flavors, showcasing the precision and artistry that defines The French Laundry. Enjoy the culinary journey!

58. "Boudin Noir"

Indulge your palate in the exquisite world of French culinary artistry with our rendition of Boudin Noir, a classic dish that pays homage to the rich traditions celebrated at Thomas Keller's renowned The French Laundry restaurant. Bursting with bold flavors and a touch of sophistication, this dish captures the essence of the culinary masterpiece that is The French Laundry.

Serving: 4 servings
Preparation Time: 20 minutes
Ready Time: 45 minutes

Ingredients:
- 1 pound (450g) fresh blood sausage (boudin noir)
- 2 tablespoons unsalted butter
- 1 large onion, finely chopped
- 2 cloves garlic, minced
- 1 cup (240ml) chicken stock
- 1/4 cup (60ml) heavy cream
- 1 teaspoon Dijon mustard
- Salt and black pepper, to taste
- Fresh parsley, chopped (for garnish)

Instructions:
1. Prepare the Blood Sausage:
- Remove the casing from the blood sausage and crumble the sausage into small pieces.
2. Sauté Onions and Garlic:
- In a large skillet, melt the butter over medium heat.
- Add the finely chopped onion and sauté until translucent.
- Stir in the minced garlic and cook until fragrant.
3. Cook the Blood Sausage:
- Add the crumbled blood sausage to the skillet, breaking it up with a spoon as it cooks.
- Cook until the sausage is browned and cooked through.
4. Deglaze with Chicken Stock:
- Pour in the chicken stock to deglaze the pan, scraping up any flavorful bits from the bottom.

- Allow the mixture to simmer for 10 minutes, allowing the flavors to meld.

5. Add Cream and Mustard:
- Stir in the heavy cream and Dijon mustard, combining well.
- Season with salt and black pepper to taste.

6. Simmer to Perfection:
- Let the mixture simmer for an additional 15 minutes, allowing the flavors to meld and the sauce to thicken.

7. Garnish and Serve:
- Garnish with fresh chopped parsley.
- Serve the Boudin Noir hot, perhaps accompanied by a side of creamy mashed potatoes or crusty French bread to savor every delectable bite.

Nutrition Information:
(Per Serving)
- Calories: 380 kcal
- Protein: 15g
- Fat: 28g
- Carbohydrates: 15g
- Fiber: 2g
- Sugar: 3g
- Sodium: 900mg

Elevate your culinary experience with this Boudin Noir recipe, capturing the essence of The French Laundry's exquisite menu. Each bite is a symphony of flavors that will transport you to the heart of French gastronomy.

59. Crispy Skin Suckling Pig

Indulge your palate in the exquisite world of culinary mastery with our rendition of Crispy Skin Suckling Pig—an homage to the unparalleled dining experience at Thomas Keller's iconic The French Laundry restaurant. Elevate your home cooking with this tantalizing recipe that captures the essence of precision, flavor, and crisp perfection. From the crackling skin to the succulent meat, this dish promises to transport you to the culinary heights inspired by one of the world's most celebrated chefs.

Serving: 4-6 servings
Preparation Time: 24 hours (including marination)
Ready Time: 5 hours

Ingredients:
- 1 suckling pig (approximately 15-20 pounds)
- 2 cups kosher salt
- 1 cup sugar
- 4 tablespoons black peppercorns
- 6 bay leaves
- 10 cloves garlic, crushed
- 4 sprigs fresh thyme
- 4 sprigs fresh rosemary
- 4 quarts water
- 2 cups rice vinegar
- 1 cup all-purpose flour
- Salt and pepper to taste

Instructions:
1. Preparation:
a. In a large pot, combine kosher salt, sugar, black peppercorns, bay leaves, crushed garlic, thyme, rosemary, water, and rice vinegar. Stir until the salt and sugar dissolve.
b. Place the suckling pig in a large container or brining bag, and pour the brine mixture over the pig. Ensure the pig is fully submerged. Refrigerate for 24 hours, turning the pig occasionally for even marination.
2. Remove and Dry:
a. Preheat the oven to 350°F (175°C).
b. Remove the suckling pig from the brine and pat it dry with paper towels, inside and out.
c. Allow the pig to air-dry in the refrigerator for an additional 4-6 hours. This step is crucial for achieving crispy skin.
3. Season and Truss:
a. Season the pig inside and out with salt and pepper.
b. Truss the pig, securing the legs and tying the arms close to the body.
4. Roasting:
a. Place the pig on a rack in a roasting pan.
b. Roast in the preheated oven for 4-5 hours or until the internal temperature reaches 160°F (71°C), basting occasionally with pan juices.
5. Crisping the Skin:

a. Increase the oven temperature to 450°F (232°C) for the last 30 minutes to crisp up the skin.
b. If needed, you can use a kitchen torch or broiler to achieve a perfect, crispy finish.
6. Rest and Serve:
a. Allow the suckling pig to rest for 20-30 minutes before carving.
b. Serve on a platter, garnished with fresh herbs.

Nutrition Information:
Note: Nutrition information is approximate and may vary based on the size of the pig and specific ingredients used.
- Calories per serving: 800
- Protein: 30g
- Carbohydrates: 5g
- Fat: 70g
- Fiber: 1g

Experience the magic of Thomas Keller's culinary world with this Crispy Skin Suckling Pig, a masterpiece that promises to make your dining table the epicenter of gourmet delight.

60. Roasted Saddle of Elysian Fields Farm Lamb

Indulge your senses in the culinary excellence of Thomas Keller's renowned The French Laundry with this exquisite recipe for Roasted Saddle of Elysian Fields Farm Lamb. A true masterpiece that captures the essence of fine dining, this dish promises a symphony of flavors and textures that will elevate your home cooking experience. Inspired by the meticulous craftsmanship of Keller's kitchen, this recipe invites you to embark on a gastronomic journey with the finest ingredients and precise techniques.

Serving: 4 servings
Preparation Time: 30 minutes
Ready Time: 2 hours (including marination and resting time)

Ingredients:
- 1 saddle of Elysian Fields Farm lamb (approximately 4 pounds)
- Salt and black pepper, to taste

- 2 tablespoons Dijon mustard
- 2 tablespoons olive oil
- 4 cloves garlic, minced
- 2 tablespoons fresh rosemary, chopped
- 1 tablespoon fresh thyme, chopped
- 1 tablespoon fresh parsley, chopped
- 1 lemon, zest and juice
- 1 cup chicken stock

Instructions:
1. Preheat the Oven:
Preheat your oven to 375°F (190°C).
2. Prepare the Lamb:
- Trim excess fat from the lamb saddle, leaving a thin layer for flavor.
- Season the lamb generously with salt and black pepper.
3. Marinate the Lamb:
- In a small bowl, combine Dijon mustard, olive oil, minced garlic, rosemary, thyme, parsley, lemon zest, and lemon juice.
- Rub the lamb thoroughly with the marinade, ensuring an even coating.
- Allow the lamb to marinate for at least 30 minutes to let the flavors meld.
4. Roast the Lamb:
- Place the marinated lamb on a roasting pan.
- Roast in the preheated oven for about 1 hour and 15 minutes or until the internal temperature reaches 130°F (54°C) for medium-rare.
- Baste the lamb with chicken stock every 20 minutes to keep it moist.
5. Rest and Carve:
- Allow the roasted lamb to rest for 15 minutes before carving.
- Slice the lamb into individual portions, serving with the pan juices.
6. Serve:
- Plate the carved lamb elegantly, drizzling with the pan juices.
- Garnish with additional fresh herbs if desired.

Nutrition Information:
Note: Nutrition information is approximate and may vary based on specific ingredients and portion sizes.
- Calories: 450 per serving
- Protein: 30g
- Carbohydrates: 2g
- Fat: 35g

- Saturated Fat: 12g
- Cholesterol: 120mg
- Sodium: 350mg
- Fiber: 1g
- Sugar: 0g

Delight in the culinary brilliance of The French Laundry as you savor every bite of this Roasted Saddle of Elysian Fields Farm Lamb, a testament to the artistry and passion that defines Thomas Keller's iconic restaurant.

61. "Gâteau Basque"

Indulge your senses in the exquisite world of French culinary mastery with our rendition of Gâteau Basque, a timeless dessert that pays homage to the rich gastronomic heritage of the Basque region. Inspired by the meticulous and innovative approach of Thomas Keller's The French Laundry, this recipe brings forth the essence of traditional flavors harmonized with modern culinary finesse. With its buttery crust and luscious filling, Gâteau Basque is a delightful symphony of textures and tastes that will transport you to the heart of France's culinary excellence.

Serving: 8-10 servings
Preparation Time: 30 minutes
Ready Time: 2 hours (including chilling and baking time)

Ingredients:
For the Dough:
- 2 cups all-purpose flour
- 1 cup unsalted butter, softened
- 3/4 cup granulated sugar
- 1 large egg
- 1/2 teaspoon salt
- Zest of one lemon

For the Filling:
- 1 1/2 cups almond flour
- 3/4 cup granulated sugar
- 1/2 cup unsalted butter, softened
- 2 large eggs

- 1 teaspoon vanilla extract
- 1/4 teaspoon salt
- 1/4 cup dark rum (optional)

Instructions:
1. Prepare the Dough:
a. In a mixing bowl, cream together the softened butter and sugar until light and fluffy.
b. Add the egg, salt, and lemon zest, and mix until well combined.
c. Gradually add the flour, mixing until a soft dough forms.
d. Divide the dough in half, shape each half into a disc, wrap in plastic wrap, and refrigerate for at least 30 minutes.
2. Make the Filling:
a. In a separate bowl, combine almond flour, sugar, softened butter, eggs, vanilla extract, salt, and rum (if using). Mix until smooth and well incorporated.
3. Assemble the Gâteau Basque:
a. Preheat the oven to 350°F (180°C).
b. Roll out one disc of the chilled dough to fit the bottom of a tart pan.
c. Spread the almond filling evenly over the dough.
d. Roll out the second disc of dough and place it on top, sealing the edges.
e. Use a knife to create a decorative pattern on the top crust.
f. Bake for 40-45 minutes or until the crust is golden brown.
g. Allow the Gâteau Basque to cool completely before serving.
4. Serve:
Gâteau Basque is traditionally served at room temperature. Slice into wedges and enjoy the delightful contrast between the crisp crust and the rich, almond-infused filling.

Nutrition Information:
(Per serving)
- Calories: 380
- Total Fat: 24g
- Saturated Fat: 12g
- Cholesterol: 90mg
- Sodium: 160mg
- Total Carbohydrates: 36g
- Dietary Fiber: 2g
- Sugars: 18g

- Protein: 6g

Elevate your dessert experience with this Gâteau Basque inspired by the culinary artistry of Thomas Keller's The French Laundry. Bon appétit!

62. "Rouelle"

Rouelle, a dish inspired by the esteemed Thomas Keller's The French Laundry, embodies the essence of classic French cuisine. This delectable pork dish, known for its succulence and rich flavors, offers a delightful balance of textures and tastes, making it a treasured choice for a memorable dining experience.

Serving: Serves: 4
Preparation Time: Preparation: 20 minutes
Ready Time: Ready in: 2 hours 30 minutes

Ingredients:
- 4 pork shoulder steaks, approximately 1 inch thick
- 2 tablespoons olive oil
- Salt and freshly ground black pepper
- 2 tablespoons Dijon mustard
- 2 tablespoons honey
- 2 cloves garlic, minced
- 1 cup chicken or vegetable broth
- 1 tablespoon butter
- Chopped fresh parsley for garnish

Instructions:
1. Preheat the oven to 325°F (165°C).
2. Season the pork shoulder steaks generously with salt and pepper on both sides.
3. In a skillet over medium-high heat, add olive oil. Once hot, sear the pork steaks for about 3-4 minutes on each side until golden brown. Remove from the skillet and place them in an ovenproof dish.
4. In a small bowl, mix the Dijon mustard, honey, and minced garlic. Spread this mixture over the top of each pork steak.
5. Pour the chicken or vegetable broth into the bottom of the ovenproof dish around the pork steaks.

6. Cover the dish with foil and place it in the preheated oven. Bake for about 2 hours, or until the pork is tender and cooked through.
7. Once the pork is cooked, remove it from the oven. Transfer the pork steaks to a serving platter and cover them loosely with foil to keep warm.
8. Place the ovenproof dish with the cooking juices on the stove over medium heat. Bring it to a simmer, stirring occasionally, until the liquid reduces slightly. Add the butter and stir until it melts and combines with the sauce.
9. Pour the sauce over the pork steaks and garnish with chopped fresh parsley before serving.

Nutrition Information:
(Per serving)
- Calories: 380
- Total Fat: 20g
- Saturated Fat: 6g
- Cholesterol: 120mg
- Sodium: 460mg
- Total Carbohydrate: 9g
- Dietary Fiber: 1g
- Sugars: 7g
- Protein: 38g

Enjoy the tender, flavorful Rouelle that pays homage to the culinary excellence of The French Laundry!

63. Coconut Sorbet

Indulge in the ethereal creaminess of Coconut Sorbet, a delightful treat inspired by the refined palate of Thomas Keller's The French Laundry. This elegant dessert balances the tropical sweetness of coconut with a refreshing twist, offering a luxurious and palate-cleansing experience after a sumptuous meal.

Serving: Serves: 6-8
Preparation Time: 15 minutes
Ready Time: Chilling: 4-6 hours

Ingredients:

- 2 cups coconut milk
- 1 cup coconut cream
- 3/4 cup granulated sugar
- 1/4 teaspoon salt
- 1 teaspoon vanilla extract
- 2 tablespoons coconut rum (optional)
- Shredded coconut or toasted coconut flakes for garnish (optional)

Instructions:
1. Preparation: In a saucepan over medium heat, combine the coconut milk, coconut cream, sugar, and salt. Stir gently until the sugar dissolves completely.
2. Infusion: Allow the mixture to simmer gently for 5-7 minutes, stirring occasionally. Remove from heat and let it cool for 10-15 minutes.
3. Flavor Enhancement (Optional): Stir in the vanilla extract and coconut rum, infusing the sorbet base with an extra layer of tropical flavor. This step is optional but highly recommended for an enhanced taste profile.
4. Chill: Transfer the mixture into a bowl, cover it, and refrigerate until thoroughly chilled, approximately 2-3 hours.
5. Churning: Pour the chilled mixture into an ice cream maker and churn according to the manufacturer's instructions until the sorbet reaches a smooth, frozen consistency, typically about 20-25 minutes.
6. Freezing: Transfer the churned sorbet into a freezer-safe container, covering it with a lid or plastic wrap. Freeze for an additional 2-3 hours until firm.
7. Serve: When ready to serve, scoop the Coconut Sorbet into chilled bowls or dessert glasses. Garnish with shredded coconut or toasted coconut flakes for an added textural and visual appeal.

Nutrition Information:
- Serving size: 1 scoop (approximately 90g)
- Calories: 160
- Total Fat: 12g
- Saturated Fat: 10g
- Cholesterol: 0mg
- Sodium: 75mg
- Total Carbohydrates: 15g
- Dietary Fiber: 1g
- Sugars: 12g
- Protein: 1g

This Coconut Sorbet is a luscious finale to any meal, providing a refreshing conclusion with its tropical essence. Adjust the sweetness to your preference and savor the delightful taste of paradise in every spoonful.

64. "Palet d'Or"

The "Palet d'Or" is an exquisite dessert that captures the essence of sophistication and indulgence, inspired by the renowned menu of Thomas Keller's The French Laundry restaurant. This delectable treat is a symphony of flavors and textures, combining rich chocolate, velvety ganache, and delicate gold leaf for a truly luxurious experience.

Serving: 6 servings
Preparation time: 30 minutes
Ready time: 3 hours (includes chilling time)

Ingredients:
- 7 ounces bittersweet chocolate, finely chopped
- 1 cup heavy cream
- 2 tablespoons unsalted butter, at room temperature
- Edible gold leaf, for garnish

Instructions:
1. Prepare the Chocolate Ganache:
- Place the chopped bittersweet chocolate in a heatproof bowl.
- In a saucepan, heat the heavy cream over medium heat until it just begins to simmer. Remove from heat.
- Pour the hot cream over the chopped chocolate. Let it sit undisturbed for 2-3 minutes to soften the chocolate.
- Gently stir the chocolate and cream together until smooth and fully combined.
- Add the room temperature butter and stir until incorporated into the ganache.
2. Assemble the Palet d'Or:
- Line a baking sheet or tray with parchment paper.
- Pour the chocolate ganache onto the prepared tray, spreading it evenly to a thickness of about 1/2 inch.

- Refrigerate the ganache for at least 2 hours or until firm.
- Once the ganache has set, use a round cookie cutter or a small glass to cut out individual rounds of the ganache. Place them on a serving platter.

3. Garnish with Gold Leaf:
- Carefully place small pieces of edible gold leaf on top of each palet d'or for a touch of elegance and visual appeal.

4. Serve:
- Plate the Palet d'Or on individual dessert plates and serve chilled.

Nutrition Information: (per serving)
Note: Nutritional values may vary based on specific ingredients used.
- Calories: Approximately 300 kcal
- Total Fat: 25g
- Saturated Fat: 15g
- Cholesterol: 45mg
- Sodium: 10mg
- Total Carbohydrates: 20g
- Dietary Fiber: 3g
- Sugars: 15g
- Protein: 3g

This dessert is a sublime finale to any meal, combining the artistry of fine dining with the pleasure of savoring every bite. Enjoy the decadence and sophistication of the Palet d'Or, a true testament to culinary excellence.

65. "Café Liégeois"

Indulge in the exquisite flavors of Café Liégeois, a classic dessert inspired by the culinary brilliance of Thomas Keller's renowned restaurant, The French Laundry. This delightful coffee-based treat is a perfect blend of rich espresso, velvety ice cream, and luscious whipped cream—a symphony of textures and tastes that elevates the dining experience to new heights. Bring a touch of French sophistication to your table with this elegant yet straightforward recipe.

Serving: 4 servings
Preparation Time: 15 minutes
Ready Time: 2 hours (includes chilling time)

Ingredients:
- 1 cup strong espresso, cooled
- 4 scoops vanilla ice cream
- 1/2 cup heavy cream
- 2 tablespoons granulated sugar
- 1 teaspoon pure vanilla extract
- 4 tablespoons chocolate shavings, for garnish

Instructions:
1. Brew the Espresso:
- Prepare a cup of strong espresso using your preferred method. Allow it to cool to room temperature.
2. Chill the Glasses:
- Place the serving glasses in the refrigerator to chill while you prepare the other components.
3. Assemble the Base:
- Once the espresso has cooled, pour an equal amount into each chilled glass.
4. Add Ice Cream:
- Place a scoop of vanilla ice cream into each glass, allowing it to float on the surface of the espresso.
5. Whip the Cream:
- In a mixing bowl, whip the heavy cream, sugar, and vanilla extract until soft peaks form.
6. Top with Whipped Cream:
- Spoon a generous dollop of the whipped cream onto each serving, creating a billowy crown.
7. Garnish with Chocolate Shavings:
- Sprinkle chocolate shavings over the whipped cream for a decadent finish.
8. Chill and Serve:
- Return the assembled Café Liégeois to the refrigerator and let it chill for at least 2 hours to allow the flavors to meld.
9. Present with Elegance:
- Just before serving, garnish with an extra sprinkle of chocolate shavings for an added touch of sophistication.

Nutrition Information:
- *Note: Nutrition values are approximate and may vary based on specific ingredients used.*

- Calories per serving: 280
- Total Fat: 18g
- Saturated Fat: 11g
- Cholesterol: 60mg
- Sodium: 50mg
- Total Carbohydrates: 24g
- Dietary Fiber: 1g
- Sugars: 20g
- Protein: 3g

Indulge in the luxurious experience of Café Liégeois—an homage to the culinary mastery of Thomas Keller and The French Laundry. This dessert is not only a treat for the taste buds but also a celebration of the artistry that defines French cuisine.

66. "Nougatine"

Indulge your senses in the exquisite world of culinary mastery with this Nougatine recipe inspired by the iconic menu of Thomas Keller's The French Laundry restaurant. Nougatine, a delicate confection of caramelized nuts and a hint of vanilla, captures the essence of sophistication and sweetness in every bite. Elevate your dining experience with this delightful treat that perfectly balances crunch and flavor.

Serving: Makes approximately 20 servings
Preparation Time: 15 minutes
Ready Time: 1 hour (including cooling time)

Ingredients:
- 1 cup sliced almonds
- 1 cup hazelnuts, chopped
- 1 cup sugar
- 1/4 cup water
- 1/2 teaspoon vanilla extract
- 1/4 teaspoon salt

Instructions:
1. Prepare the Nuts:

- Preheat the oven to 350°F (175°C).
- Spread the sliced almonds and chopped hazelnuts on a baking sheet in a single layer.
- Toast the nuts in the preheated oven for about 8-10 minutes or until they turn golden brown. Keep a close eye on them to prevent burning.

2. Make the Caramel:
- In a medium-sized saucepan, combine sugar and water over medium heat.
- Stir until the sugar dissolves, then let it come to a boil. Allow the mixture to boil without stirring until it reaches a rich amber color.

3. Combine and Flavor:
- Once the caramel is ready, remove the saucepan from heat.
- Quickly stir in the toasted nuts, vanilla extract, and salt until well combined.

4. Shape the Nougatine:
- Working swiftly, pour the caramel-nut mixture onto a parchment-lined baking sheet.
- Using a spatula or the back of a spoon, spread the mixture into an even layer.

5. Cool and Break:
- Allow the nougatine to cool completely at room temperature or in the refrigerator.
- Once cooled and hardened, break the nougatine into bite-sized pieces.

6. Serve:
- Arrange the Nougatine pieces on a decorative platter and serve as a delightful treat with coffee or as a sweet ending to a luxurious meal.

Nutrition Information:
Note: Nutrition information is approximate and may vary based on specific ingredients and portion sizes.
- Serving Size: 1 piece
- Calories: 80
- Total Fat: 5g
- Saturated Fat: 0.4g
- Trans Fat: 0g
- Cholesterol: 0mg
- Sodium: 30mg
- Total Carbohydrates: 8g
- Dietary Fiber: 1g
- Sugars: 6g

- Protein: 2g

Indulge in the divine symphony of caramelized nuts and vanilla with this Nougatine recipe, a tribute to the culinary excellence of Thomas Keller's The French Laundry. Elevate your dessert experience with this delicate and crunchy delight.

67. "Profiteroles"

Indulge in the exquisite world of French culinary artistry with these delightful Profiteroles, a classic pastry treat that encapsulates the essence of Thomas Keller's renowned The French Laundry restaurant. These golden orbs of choux pastry are filled with luscious cream and adorned with a decadent chocolate sauce—a dessert that transcends simplicity to achieve unparalleled elegance.

Serving: Makes approximately 20 profiteroles.
Preparation Time: 20 minutes.
Ready Time: 2 hours.

Ingredients:
For the Choux Pastry:
- 1 cup water
- 1/2 cup unsalted butter
- 1/4 teaspoon salt
- 1 cup all-purpose flour
- 4 large eggs

For the Vanilla Cream Filling:
- 2 cups heavy cream
- 1/2 cup granulated sugar
- 1 teaspoon vanilla extract

For the Chocolate Sauce:
- 4 ounces dark chocolate, finely chopped
- 1/2 cup heavy cream
- 2 tablespoons unsalted butter
- 2 tablespoons powdered sugar

Instructions:
Choux Pastry:

1. In a medium saucepan, bring water, butter, and salt to a boil over medium heat.
2. Add the flour all at once, stirring vigorously with a wooden spoon until the mixture forms a smooth ball and pulls away from the sides of the pan.
3. Remove from heat and let the mixture cool for a few minutes.
4. Add eggs one at a time, beating well after each addition until the dough is smooth.
5. Preheat the oven to 425°F (220°C) and line a baking sheet with parchment paper.
6. Transfer the choux pastry to a pastry bag fitted with a large round tip and pipe small mounds onto the prepared baking sheet.
7. Bake for 15 minutes, then reduce the oven temperature to 375°F (190°C) and bake for an additional 15 minutes or until golden brown.
8. Remove from the oven and let the profiteroles cool completely.

Vanilla Cream Filling:
1. In a mixing bowl, whip the heavy cream, sugar, and vanilla extract until stiff peaks form.
2. Slice the cooled profiteroles in half and fill each with a generous dollop of vanilla cream.

Chocolate Sauce:
1. In a heatproof bowl, melt the dark chocolate, heavy cream, and butter over a double boiler.
2. Once melted, whisk in the powdered sugar until smooth.
3. Drizzle the chocolate sauce over the assembled profiteroles.

Nutrition Information:
(Per serving - 1 profiterole)
- Calories: 180
- Total Fat: 14g
- Saturated Fat: 8g
- Trans Fat: 0g
- Cholesterol: 70mg
- Sodium: 45mg
- Total Carbohydrates: 11g
- Dietary Fiber: 1g
- Sugars: 6g
- Protein: 2g

Embrace the culinary finesse of The French Laundry with these Profiteroles—a symphony of textures and flavors that will elevate any dining experience. Enjoy the delicate balance of the crisp choux pastry, velvety vanilla cream, and rich chocolate sauce, transporting your taste buds to the heart of French gastronomy.

68. "Kaffir Lime"

Elevate your culinary experience with the vibrant and aromatic flavors of Kaffir Lime, a key ingredient in Thomas Keller's renowned restaurant, The French Laundry. This citrus gem adds a unique zest to dishes, creating a symphony of tastes that dance on your palate. In this recipe, we explore the essence of Kaffir Lime in a dish inspired by the unparalleled menu of The French Laundry.

Serving: 4 servings
Preparation Time: 15 minutes
Ready Time: 45 minutes

Ingredients:
- 1 lb (450g) chicken breast, thinly sliced
- 2 tablespoons vegetable oil
- 1 red bell pepper, julienned
- 1 yellow bell pepper, julienned
- 1 cup snap peas, ends trimmed
- 2 cloves garlic, minced
- 1 tablespoon fresh ginger, grated
- Zest of 2 Kaffir Limes
- 2 tablespoons Kaffir Lime juice
- 3 tablespoons soy sauce
- 1 tablespoon fish sauce
- 1 tablespoon honey
- 1 teaspoon cornstarch, dissolved in 2 tablespoons water
- Fresh cilantro leaves for garnish
- Cooked jasmine rice for serving

Instructions:
1. Heat the vegetable oil in a wok or large skillet over medium-high heat.
2. Add the sliced chicken to the pan and cook until browned and cooked through. Remove chicken from the pan and set aside.

3. In the same pan, add a bit more oil if needed. Sauté the garlic and ginger until fragrant.
4. Add the julienned bell peppers and snap peas to the pan, stir-frying until they are slightly tender but still crisp.
5. In a small bowl, mix together the Kaffir Lime zest, Kaffir Lime juice, soy sauce, fish sauce, honey, and the dissolved cornstarch. Pour this sauce over the vegetables in the pan.
6. Return the cooked chicken to the pan and toss everything together until the sauce thickens and coats the ingredients evenly.
7. Serve the Kaffir Lime chicken over jasmine rice, garnished with fresh cilantro leaves.

Nutrition Information (per serving):
- Calories: 350
- Protein: 25g
- Carbohydrates: 30g
- Fat: 15g
- Fiber: 4g
- Sugar: 8g
- Sodium: 800mg

Elevate your dining experience with the tantalizing flavors of Kaffir Lime, inspired by the culinary excellence of Thomas Keller's The French Laundry. This dish is a celebration of freshness and sophistication, bringing the essence of this distinguished restaurant into your own kitchen.

69. "Baba au Rhum"

Indulge in the decadent world of French culinary excellence with our take on the classic dessert, "Baba au Rhum." This exquisite creation draws inspiration from the impeccable menu of Thomas Keller's renowned restaurant, The French Laundry. Immerse yourself in the rich flavors and velvety textures of this delightful treat, where every bite is a symphony of taste and elegance.

Serving: Serves 8
Preparation Time: 30 minutes
Ready Time: 4 hours (including chilling and soaking time)

Ingredients:
For the Baba:
- 2 1/4 teaspoons active dry yeast
- 1/4 cup warm water (110°F/43°C)
- 3 cups all-purpose flour
- 1/2 teaspoon salt
- 1/4 cup granulated sugar
- 4 large eggs
- 1/2 cup whole milk
- 1/2 cup unsalted butter, softened

For the Rum Syrup:
- 1 cup water
- 1 cup granulated sugar
- 1 cup dark rum

For Serving:
- Freshly whipped cream
- Mixed berries

Instructions:
1. Prepare the Baba:
a. In a small bowl, combine the warm water and yeast. Let it sit for 5 minutes until it becomes frothy.
b. In a large mixing bowl, whisk together the flour, salt, and sugar.
c. Make a well in the center of the dry ingredients and add the yeast mixture, eggs, and milk. Mix until a soft dough forms.
d. Add the softened butter and knead the dough until smooth and elastic.
e. Cover the bowl with plastic wrap and let the dough rise in a warm place for 1-2 hours, or until it doubles in size.
2. Shape and Bake:
a. Preheat the oven to 375°F (190°C).
b. Grease a Baba mold or individual molds.
c. Punch down the risen dough and fill each mold about halfway.
d. Bake for 15-20 minutes or until golden brown.
e. Remove from the oven and let the Babas cool in the molds for 10 minutes before transferring to a wire rack.
3. Prepare the Rum Syrup:
a. In a saucepan, combine water and sugar. Bring to a simmer, stirring until the sugar dissolves.
b. Remove from heat and stir in the dark rum.

4. Soak the Babas:
a. Once the Babas have cooled, place them in a shallow dish and generously brush with the rum syrup. Allow them to soak for at least 2 hours, turning occasionally.
5. Serve:
a. Plate the Babas and garnish with freshly whipped cream and mixed berries.

Nutrition Information (per serving):
(Note: Nutritional values may vary based on specific ingredients and serving sizes.)
- Calories: 350
- Total Fat: 15g
- Saturated Fat: 9g
- Cholesterol: 110mg
- Sodium: 120mg
- Total Carbohydrates: 42g
- Dietary Fiber: 1g
- Sugars: 20g
- Protein: 6g

Embrace the opulence of The French Laundry's culinary legacy with this Baba au Rhum recipe, a dessert that captures the essence of sophisticated sweetness. Enjoy the luscious interplay of textures and the warming notes of rum, making every bite a celebration of indulgence.

70. "Religieuse"

The Religieuse, a delightful French pastry, is a true testament to the artistry and precision celebrated in Thomas Keller's renowned restaurant, The French Laundry. This delicate confection is composed of two cream-filled choux pastry puffs, one perched atop the other, resembling a nun in a habit – hence the name "Religieuse," meaning nun in French. The craftsmanship and flavors of this dessert epitomize the culinary excellence that defines The French Laundry's menu. Embark on a culinary journey with this exquisite pastry that pays homage to the precision and creativity of Thomas Keller's iconic cuisine.

Serving: 4 servings

Preparation Time: 30 minutes
Ready Time: 2 hours (including chilling time)

Ingredients:
For the Choux Pastry:
- 1/2 cup water
- 1/2 cup whole milk
- 1/2 cup unsalted butter, cut into small pieces
- 1 tablespoon granulated sugar
- 1/4 teaspoon salt
- 1 cup all-purpose flour
- 4 large eggs

For the Pastry Cream:
- 2 cups whole milk
- 1/2 cup granulated sugar
- 4 large egg yolks
- 1/4 cup cornstarch
- 1 teaspoon vanilla extract

For the Chocolate Glaze:
- 4 ounces dark chocolate, chopped
- 1/2 cup heavy cream
- 2 tablespoons unsalted butter

Instructions:
1. *Prepare Choux Pastry:*
a. In a saucepan, combine water, milk, butter, sugar, and salt. Bring to a simmer over medium heat.
b. Add flour all at once and stir vigorously with a wooden spoon until the mixture forms a ball and pulls away from the sides.
c. Transfer the mixture to a bowl and let it cool for a few minutes. Add eggs one at a time, beating well after each addition until smooth.
d. Preheat the oven to 400°F (200°C). Pipe or spoon small mounds of dough onto a baking sheet.
e. Bake for 20-25 minutes or until golden brown. Let cool completely.

2. *Prepare Pastry Cream:*
a. In a saucepan, heat the milk until it simmers. In a bowl, whisk together sugar, egg yolks, and cornstarch until smooth.
b. Slowly pour the hot milk into the egg mixture, whisking constantly. Return the mixture to the saucepan and cook over medium heat until thickened.

c. Remove from heat, stir in vanilla extract, and let it cool completely.
3. *Assemble Religieuse:*
a. Cut each choux pastry puff in half horizontally. Fill a piping bag with pastry cream and pipe onto the bottom half of each puff.
b. Place the top half of each puff over the cream, creating a stack. Repeat with the remaining puffs.
4. *Prepare Chocolate Glaze:*
a. In a heatproof bowl, combine chopped chocolate, heavy cream, and butter. Melt over a double boiler or in the microwave, stirring until smooth.
b. Dip the top of each Religieuse into the chocolate glaze, allowing excess to drip off.
5. *Chill:*
a. Place the Religieuse in the refrigerator for at least 1 hour to allow the chocolate glaze to set and the flavors to meld.

Nutrition Information:
(Per Serving)
Calories: 450
Fat: 30g
Saturated Fat: 18g
Cholesterol: 215mg
Sodium: 150mg
Carbohydrates: 38g
Fiber: 2g
Sugar: 20g
Protein: 9g
Indulge in the divine taste of the Religieuse, a masterpiece inspired by the culinary brilliance of Thomas Keller's The French Laundry. This intricate dessert is sure to captivate your senses and elevate your appreciation for the art of French pastry-making.

71. "Pavlova"

Indulge your taste buds in the ethereal world of desserts with this exquisite Pavlova, inspired by the culinary artistry of Thomas Keller's The French Laundry. Named after the Russian ballerina Anna Pavlova, this delicate meringue-based dessert boasts a crisp exterior and a marshmallow-soft interior. Paired with luscious whipped cream and an abundance of fresh, vibrant fruits, this Pavlova is a symphony of textures and flavors that will transport you to the heights of culinary delight.

Serving: Serves 8
Preparation Time: 20 minutes
Ready Time: 2 hours (including baking and cooling time)

Ingredients:
- 4 large egg whites, at room temperature
- 1 cup granulated sugar
- 1 teaspoon white vinegar
- 1 teaspoon cornstarch
- 1 teaspoon vanilla extract
- 1 cup heavy cream
- 2 tablespoons powdered sugar
- Fresh berries (strawberries, blueberries, raspberries) for topping

Instructions:
1. Preheat the oven to 300°F (150°C) and line a baking sheet with parchment paper.
2. In a clean, dry bowl, whip the egg whites with an electric mixer until soft peaks form.
3. Gradually add the granulated sugar, one tablespoon at a time, while continuing to whip the egg whites. Whip until glossy and stiff peaks form.
4. Gently fold in the white vinegar, cornstarch, and vanilla extract.
5. Spoon the meringue onto the prepared baking sheet, creating a circular shape with a slight indentation in the center.
6. Bake in the preheated oven for 1 hour and 30 minutes, or until the Pavlova has a crisp exterior and is dry to the touch.
7. Turn off the oven and leave the Pavlova inside to cool completely.
8. In a separate bowl, whip the heavy cream and powdered sugar until soft peaks form.
9. Carefully transfer the cooled Pavlova to a serving platter, fill the center with the whipped cream, and top with an assortment of fresh berries.
10. Serve immediately and savor the divine combination of crispy meringue, velvety cream, and the burst of fruity freshness.

Nutrition Information:

Per serving
- Calories: 250
- Fat: 15g
- Carbohydrates: 28g
- Protein: 3g
- Fiber: 2g
- Sugar: 25g

Elevate your dessert experience with this Pavlova, a masterpiece inspired by the culinary excellence of Thomas Keller's The French Laundry.

72. "Savarin au Mille-Feuille"

Savarin au Mille-Feuille is a delightful dessert that pays homage to the exquisite French culinary tradition. Inspired by the masterful creations of Thomas Keller's The French Laundry, this recipe combines the lightness of a classic Savarin with the delicate layers of a Mille-Feuille, resulting in a dessert that is as visually stunning as it is delicious. The harmonious marriage of textures and flavors in this dish is sure to elevate any dining experience.

Serving: 4 servings
Preparation Time: 30 minutes
Ready Time: 3 hours (includes chilling time)

Ingredients:
- For the Savarin:
- 1 cup all-purpose flour
- 1/4 cup granulated sugar
- 1 tablespoon active dry yeast
- 1/2 cup warm milk
- 3 large eggs
- 1/2 cup unsalted butter, softened
- 1 teaspoon vanilla extract
- For the Mille-Feuille Layers:
- 1 sheet puff pastry, thawed if frozen
- 1/4 cup powdered sugar for dusting
- For the Diplomat Cream:
- 1 cup whole milk

- 3 large egg yolks
- 1/2 cup granulated sugar
- 2 tablespoons cornstarch
- 1 teaspoon vanilla extract
- 1 cup heavy cream, whipped

Instructions:
1. Prepare the Savarin:
- In a small bowl, combine the warm milk and active dry yeast. Let it sit for 5 minutes until frothy.
- In a large mixing bowl, whisk together the flour and sugar. Add the yeast mixture, eggs, softened butter, and vanilla extract. Mix until a smooth batter forms.
- Grease a Savarin mold and pour the batter into it. Let it rise in a warm place for about 1-2 hours or until doubled in size.
- Preheat the oven to 350°F (180°C) and bake the Savarin for 20-25 minutes or until golden brown. Allow it to cool completely.
2. Prepare the Mille-Feuille Layers:
- Roll out the puff pastry sheet on a floured surface. Cut it into rectangular pieces.
- Place the pastry pieces on a baking sheet and bake according to the package instructions until golden and puffed.
- Once cooled, dust the pastry pieces with powdered sugar.
3. Prepare the Diplomat Cream:
- In a saucepan, heat the milk until it simmers. In a separate bowl, whisk together the egg yolks, sugar, and cornstarch.
- Slowly pour the hot milk into the egg mixture, whisking constantly. Return the mixture to the saucepan and cook over medium heat until thickened.
- Remove from heat, stir in the vanilla extract, and let it cool. Once cooled, fold in the whipped cream.
4. Assemble the Savarin au Mille-Feuille:
- Cut the Savarin in half horizontally. Place one half on a serving platter.
- Layer the Mille-Feuille rectangles on top, spreading a generous amount of Diplomat Cream between each layer.
- Top with the second half of the Savarin.
- Garnish with additional Diplomat Cream and dust with powdered sugar.
5. Chill and Serve:

- Refrigerate the assembled Savarin au Mille-Feuille for at least 2 hours to allow the flavors to meld.
- Serve chilled and enjoy the delightful layers of flavor and texture.

Nutrition Information:
(Note: Nutrition information is approximate and may vary based on specific ingredients and serving sizes.)
- Calories per serving: 450
- Protein: 8g
- Carbohydrates: 35g
- Fat: 30g
- Fiber: 1g

Indulge in the culinary finesse of Thomas Keller's influence with this Savarin au Mille-Feuille—a dessert that embodies the artistry and precision of French cuisine.

73. "Mille-Feuille"

Indulge in the culinary elegance inspired by Thomas Keller's iconic restaurant, The French Laundry, with our exquisite Mille-Feuille recipe. This classic French pastry, meaning "a thousand layers," is a symphony of delicate puff pastry, velvety pastry cream, and a glossy layer of sweet icing. Elevate your home cooking experience with this decadent dessert that embodies the sophistication of French cuisine.

Serving: Makes 6 servings
Preparation Time: 30 minutes
Ready Time: 2 hours (including chilling time)

Ingredients:
For the Puff Pastry:
- 1 sheet store-bought puff pastry, thawed
- 1 tablespoon confectioners' sugar (for dusting)
For the Pastry Cream:
- 2 cups whole milk
- 1 vanilla bean, split lengthwise
- 6 large egg yolks
- 1/2 cup granulated sugar

- 1/3 cup cornstarch
- Pinch of salt

For the Icing:
- 1 cup confectioners' sugar
- 2 tablespoons water
- 1/2 teaspoon vanilla extract
- A pinch of salt

Instructions:
Puff Pastry:
1. Preheat your oven to 400°F (200°C).
2. Roll out the puff pastry sheet on a lightly floured surface to about 1/8-inch thickness.
3. Cut the pastry into 3x3-inch squares and place them on a parchment-lined baking sheet.
4. Prick each square with a fork to prevent excessive puffing.
5. Bake for 12-15 minutes or until golden brown and puffed.
6. Allow the pastry squares to cool completely before assembling.

Pastry Cream:
1. In a saucepan, heat the milk and vanilla bean over medium heat until it just begins to simmer. Remove from heat and let it steep for 15 minutes.
2. In a mixing bowl, whisk together the egg yolks, sugar, cornstarch, and a pinch of salt until smooth.
3. Gradually whisk the warm milk into the egg mixture. Return the mixture to the saucepan.
4. Cook over medium heat, whisking constantly until the mixture thickens and comes to a boil.
5. Remove from heat, discard the vanilla bean, and transfer the pastry cream to a bowl. Cover with plastic wrap, ensuring it touches the surface of the cream to prevent a skin from forming.
6. Chill in the refrigerator for at least 1 hour.

Icing:
1. In a bowl, whisk together confectioners' sugar, water, vanilla extract, and a pinch of salt until smooth.

Assembly:
1. Place one puff pastry square on a serving plate. Pipe or spread a layer of pastry cream on top.
2. Add another puff pastry square and repeat the process until you have three layers of pastry and two layers of cream.
3. Drizzle the icing over the top layer of the Mille-Feuille.

4. Dust with confectioners' sugar for a finishing touch.

Nutrition Information (per serving):
- Calories: 380
- Fat: 22g
- Saturated Fat: 7g
- Cholesterol: 190mg
- Sodium: 180mg
- Carbohydrates: 39g
- Fiber: 1g
- Sugars: 22g
- Protein: 7g

Indulge in the layers of luxury with this Mille-Feuille, a masterpiece inspired by the culinary excellence of The French Laundry.

74. "Meringue"

Meringue, with its delicate and airy texture, embodies the finesse and elegance synonymous with The French Laundry's exquisite menu. This sweet confection, made from simple ingredients, showcases the artistry of French pastry techniques. A crisp exterior gives way to a light, melt-in-your-mouth center, making it a delightful treat on its own or a perfect accompaniment to various desserts.

Serving: Serves: 6-8
Serve meringues as a standalone dessert or use them as a topping for pies, cakes, or fruit compotes for an added touch of sweetness and texture.
Preparation Time: 20 minutes
Ready Time: 2 hours

Ingredients:
- 4 large egg whites, at room temperature
- 1 cup granulated sugar
- Pinch of cream of tartar
- 1 teaspoon vanilla extract
- Optional: Food coloring or flavored extracts for variation

Instructions:
1. Preheat the oven to 200°F (93°C). Line a baking sheet with parchment paper.
2. In a clean, dry mixing bowl, beat the egg whites on medium speed until frothy.
3. Add the cream of tartar and continue to beat until soft peaks form.
4. Gradually add the sugar, a spoonful at a time, while continuing to beat the egg whites. Increase the speed to high and beat until stiff, glossy peaks form.
5. Gently fold in the vanilla extract (and any optional coloring or flavoring) until evenly incorporated.
6. Using a piping bag fitted with a star tip or a spoon, create mounds or shapes of meringue on the prepared baking sheet.
7. Place the baking sheet in the oven and bake for about 1.5 to 2 hours, or until the meringues are dry, crisp, and easily lift off the parchment paper.
8. Once baked, turn off the oven and let the meringues cool completely inside the oven with the door slightly ajar.
9. Store the cooled meringues in an airtight container at room temperature for up to a week.

Nutrition Information (per serving, based on 8 servings):
- Calories: 97 kcal
- Carbohydrates: 24g
- Fat: 0g
- Protein: 2g
- Sugar: 24g
- Sodium: 16mg
- Note: Nutritional values may vary depending on serving size and ingredients used.

Enjoy the lightness and sweetness of these delightful meringues, a true testament to the delicate artistry celebrated at The French Laundry.

75. "Macaron"

Macarons are delicate, airy confections that epitomize elegance and precision in French pastry-making. This recipe captures the essence of The French Laundry's finesse, blending simplicity with sophistication.

Mastering the art of macaron-making may take practice, but the result is a delightful treat that embodies the essence of this renowned restaurant's menu.

Serving: 20-24 macarons
Preparation Time: 45 minutes
Ready Time: 1 hour 30 minutes

Ingredients:
- 200g almond flour
- 200g powdered sugar
- 150g egg whites (divided into two portions of 75g each)
- 200g granulated sugar
- 50ml water
- Food coloring (optional)
- Flavored extracts or fillings of your choice (e.g., ganache, buttercream, jam)

Instructions:
1. Prepare Almond Mixture:
- Sift almond flour and powdered sugar together into a bowl.
- In another bowl, add 75g of egg whites and mix them into the almond-sugar mixture until a paste forms. Add food coloring and flavor extracts, if desired. Set aside.
2. Make the Meringue:
- In a saucepan, combine granulated sugar and water. Heat on medium-high until it reaches 118°C (244°F) on a candy thermometer.
- Meanwhile, start whipping the remaining 75g of egg whites in a clean, dry mixing bowl until soft peaks form.
- When the sugar syrup reaches 118°C (244°F), slowly pour it into the whipped egg whites while continuing to beat at medium speed. Increase speed to high and beat until stiff, glossy peaks form and the meringue has cooled.
3. Combine Mixtures:
- Gently fold the meringue into the almond mixture in three additions until the batter flows like magma. Be careful not to overmix.
4. Pipe and Rest:
- Fill a piping bag with the batter fitted with a round tip. Pipe small rounds onto parchment-lined baking sheets. Tap the baking sheets gently on the counter to release any air bubbles.

- Let the piped macarons sit at room temperature for about 30-45 minutes until a skin forms on top and they are no longer sticky to the touch.

5. Bake:
- Preheat the oven to 150°C (300°F). Bake the macarons, one sheet at a time, for 12-15 minutes, rotating the sheet halfway through. They should have formed "feet" and be set but not browned.

6. Assemble:
- Once cooled, pair similar-sized macaron shells together. Pipe or spoon your desired filling onto one shell and gently sandwich with another.

Nutrition Information (per serving, based on 1 macaron):
- Calories: 100
- Total Fat: 4g
- Saturated Fat: 0.3g
- Cholesterol: 0mg
- Sodium: 5mg
- Total Carbohydrates: 15g
- Dietary Fiber: 1g
- Sugars: 14g
- Protein: 2g

Enjoy these delightful macarons as a luxurious treat, perfect for indulging in the artistry of French pastry.

76. "Canele"

The canelé, a delightful French pastry, embodies a harmonious blend of a crisp caramelized crust and a tender custard-like interior. Inspired by the exquisite menu of Thomas Keller's The French Laundry restaurant, this recipe brings forth the irresistible allure of these small, cylindrical pastries, perfect for indulging in a taste of French sophistication at home.

Serving: This recipe yields approximately 12 canelés, ideal for sharing as a sweet treat after a meal or as an elegant addition to a brunch spread.
Preparation time: 25 minutes
Ready time: 1 hour 30 minutes (plus overnight resting time for the batter)

Ingredients:
- 2 cups whole milk
- 2 tablespoons unsalted butter
- 1 vanilla bean, split lengthwise
- 1 cup granulated sugar
- 4 large eggs
- 1 cup all-purpose flour
- 1/4 teaspoon salt
- 1/4 cup dark rum
- Butter or cooking spray (for greasing molds)

Instructions:
1. In a saucepan over medium heat, combine the whole milk, butter, and the seeds scraped from the vanilla bean. Heat the mixture until it just begins to simmer, then remove it from the heat and let it cool to room temperature.
2. In a mixing bowl, whisk together the sugar and eggs until well combined. Gradually add the flour and salt, whisking continuously to form a smooth batter.
3. Slowly pour the cooled milk mixture into the batter while whisking constantly to prevent lumps from forming. Stir in the dark rum, ensuring it's evenly incorporated.
4. Cover the batter and refrigerate it for at least 24 hours or up to 48 hours. This resting period allows the flavors to meld and develop.
5. When ready to bake, preheat the oven to 450°F (230°C). Grease the canelé molds generously with butter or cooking spray.
6. Fill each mold almost to the top with the rested batter. Place the molds on a baking sheet and bake in the preheated oven for 15 minutes.
7. After 15 minutes, reduce the oven temperature to 375°F (190°C) and continue baking for an additional 45 minutes, or until the canelés develop a deep caramelized crust.
8. Once baked, remove the canelés from the oven and let them cool in the molds for a few minutes before gently unmolding them. Allow them to cool completely on a wire rack before serving.

Nutrition Information:
(Note: Nutritional values may vary based on specific ingredients used and serving sizes.)
- Serving size: 1 canelé
- Calories: Approximately 150

- Fat: 5g
- Carbohydrates: 20g
- Protein: 4g

Enjoy these delectable canelés as a delightful finale to a meal or as a luxurious afternoon treat, embracing the essence of French pastry-making crafted from the inspiration of The French Laundry's refined menu.

77. "Tarte au Citron"

Indulge your senses with the exquisite flavors of Tarte au Citron, a classic French dessert that captures the essence of sophistication and simplicity. This recipe, inspired by the culinary brilliance of Thomas Keller's renowned restaurant, The French Laundry, promises a perfect balance of tartness and sweetness in every bite. Elevate your dining experience with this elegant lemon tart that pays homage to the timeless traditions of French pastry.

Serving: Serves 8
Preparation Time: 30 minutes
Ready Time: 3 hours (includes chilling time)

Ingredients:
For the Tart Crust:
- 1 1/2 cups all-purpose flour
- 1/2 cup unsalted butter, cold and diced
- 1/4 cup granulated sugar
- 1/4 teaspoon salt
- 1 large egg yolk
- 2 tablespoons ice water
For the Lemon Filling:
- 4 large eggs
- 1 cup granulated sugar
- 1 cup freshly squeezed lemon juice
- 1 tablespoon lemon zest
- 1/2 cup unsalted butter, melted
For Garnish (optional):
- Powdered sugar

- Fresh mint leaves

Instructions:

Tart Crust:
1. In a food processor, combine flour, cold diced butter, sugar, and salt. Pulse until the mixture resembles coarse crumbs.
2. Add the egg yolk and ice water. Pulse until the dough comes together.
3. Turn the dough out onto a floured surface and knead it into a smooth ball. Flatten into a disc, wrap in plastic wrap, and refrigerate for at least 30 minutes.
4. Preheat the oven to 375°F (190°C). Roll out the chilled dough on a floured surface and fit it into a 9-inch tart pan. Trim any excess dough.
5. Prick the bottom of the crust with a fork, line it with parchment paper, and fill it with pie weights or dried beans. Bake for 15 minutes, then remove the weights and parchment and bake for an additional 10 minutes, or until golden brown. Allow to cool.

Lemon Filling:
1. In a bowl, whisk together eggs and sugar until well combined.
2. Add the lemon juice, lemon zest, and melted butter. Whisk until smooth.
3. Pour the lemon filling into the pre-baked tart crust.
4. Bake the tart at 325°F (163°C) for 25-30 minutes or until the filling is set.
5. Allow the tart to cool to room temperature, then refrigerate for at least 2 hours before serving.

Garnish (optional):
1. Dust the chilled tart with powdered sugar just before serving.
2. Garnish with fresh mint leaves for a touch of freshness.

Nutrition Information (per serving):
- Calories: 380
- Fat: 22g
- Saturated Fat: 13g
- Cholesterol: 145mg
- Sodium: 80mg
- Carbohydrates: 42g
- Sugar: 28g
- Protein: 5g

Elevate your dessert table with this Tarte au Citron inspired by the culinary wonders of The French Laundry. Enjoy the perfect harmony of citrusy goodness and buttery crust—a true celebration of French pastry excellence.

78. "Charlotte Russe"

Celebrate the exquisite flavors of Thomas Keller's The French Laundry with this delightful recipe inspired by the renowned restaurant's menu. The Charlotte Russe is a classic French dessert that combines layers of ladyfingers or sponge cake with a velvety Bavarian cream, creating a symphony of textures and tastes that are sure to elevate any dining experience.

Serving: 8 servings
Preparation Time: 30 minutes
Ready Time: 4 hours (including chilling time)

Ingredients:
- 1 1/2 cups heavy cream
- 1/2 cup whole milk
- 1 vanilla bean, split and seeds scraped
- 4 large egg yolks
- 1/2 cup granulated sugar
- 2 teaspoons gelatin powder
- 3 tablespoons cold water
- 2 cups ladyfingers or sponge cake, sliced
- 1/4 cup apricot jam, warmed
- Fresh berries for garnish (optional)
- Mint leaves for garnish (optional)

Instructions:
1. Prepare the Bavarian Cream:
- In a saucepan, heat the heavy cream, whole milk, vanilla bean, and seeds over medium heat. Bring it to a simmer, then remove from heat and let it steep for 15 minutes.
- In a separate bowl, whisk together the egg yolks and granulated sugar until pale and thick.

- Remove the vanilla bean from the cream mixture and reheat it until it's warm. Slowly pour the warm cream into the egg mixture, whisking constantly.
- Transfer the mixture back to the saucepan and cook over low heat, stirring continuously, until the custard coats the back of a spoon. Do not let it boil.
- Dissolve gelatin in cold water and add it to the custard, stirring until well combined.
- Strain the custard through a fine-mesh sieve into a bowl, cover with plastic wrap, and refrigerate until set, about 2 hours.

2. Assemble the Charlotte Russe:
- Line the bottom of a charlotte mold or a deep cake pan with ladyfingers or sponge cake slices.
- Brush the ladyfingers or cake with warmed apricot jam.
- Pour the chilled Bavarian cream over the ladyfingers, spreading it evenly.
- Top with another layer of ladyfingers or sponge cake, pressing down gently.
- Refrigerate for at least 2 hours to allow the flavors to meld and the dessert to set.

3. Serve:
- Once ready, carefully unmold the Charlotte Russe onto a serving platter.
- Garnish with fresh berries and mint leaves if desired.

Nutrition Information:
(Per serving)
- Calories: 350
- Total Fat: 22g
- Saturated Fat: 13g
- Cholesterol: 175mg
- Sodium: 50mg
- Total Carbohydrates: 31g
- Sugars: 20g
- Protein: 5g

Indulge in the sophistication of The French Laundry with this Charlotte Russe, a dessert that embodies the essence of fine dining.

79. "Pots de Crème"

Indulge in the epitome of French elegance with our exquisite Pots de Crème recipe—a velvety custard that pays homage to the sophisticated flavors found in Thomas Keller's renowned The French Laundry restaurant. This luscious dessert, with its smooth texture and rich taste, is the perfect finale to a fine dining experience or a delightful treat for any special occasion.

Serving: This recipe makes 6 servings of Pots de Crème.
Preparation Time: 20 minutes
Ready Time: 4 hours (including chilling time)

Ingredients:
- 2 cups heavy cream
- 1 cup whole milk
- 1 vanilla bean, split lengthwise, seeds scraped out
- 6 large egg yolks
- 1/2 cup granulated sugar
- Pinch of salt
- 6 ounces bittersweet chocolate, finely chopped

Instructions:
1. Preheat the Oven:
Preheat your oven to 325°F (163°C). Place six ramekins in a baking dish, ensuring they fit comfortably with some space between them.
2. Prepare the Custard Base:
In a saucepan, combine the heavy cream, whole milk, vanilla bean, and its seeds. Heat the mixture over medium heat until it begins to simmer. Remove from heat and let it steep for about 15 minutes to infuse the vanilla flavor.
3. Whisk the Egg Yolks:
In a heatproof bowl, whisk together the egg yolks, sugar, and a pinch of salt until the mixture is pale and slightly thickened.
4. Temper the Eggs:
Gradually pour the warm milk and cream mixture into the egg yolk mixture, whisking continuously. This process, known as tempering, prevents the eggs from curdling.
5. Add the Chocolate:

Place the finely chopped bittersweet chocolate in another bowl. Pour the warm custard mixture over the chocolate and let it sit for a minute. Then, whisk until the chocolate is fully melted and the mixture is smooth.

6. Strain the Mixture:

Strain the custard through a fine-mesh sieve into a pouring jug, discarding the vanilla bean. This step ensures a silky-smooth texture.

7. Fill the Ramekins:

Pour the custard evenly into the prepared ramekins.

8. Create a Water Bath:

Fill the baking dish with hot water until it reaches halfway up the sides of the ramekins. This water bath helps the custards cook gently and evenly.

9. Bake:

Carefully transfer the baking dish to the preheated oven and bake for approximately 35-40 minutes or until the edges are set, but the center still jiggles slightly.

10. Chill:

Allow the pots de crème to cool to room temperature, then refrigerate for at least 3 hours or until fully set.

11. Serve:

Garnish with a dollop of whipped cream or a sprinkle of cocoa powder before serving.

Nutrition Information:

Note: Nutritional values are approximate and may vary based on specific ingredients used.
- Calories per serving: 450
- Total Fat: 35g
- Saturated Fat: 21g
- Cholesterol: 235mg
- Sodium: 55mg
- Total Carbohydrates: 30g
- Dietary Fiber: 2g
- Sugars: 25g
- Protein: 6g

Savor the decadence of The French Laundry with each spoonful of this Pots de Crème, a dessert that captures the essence of fine French cuisine in the comfort of your own home.

80. "Tarte Tatin"

Indulge in the exquisite flavors of French cuisine with our rendition of Tarte Tatin, a classic dessert that pays homage to the culinary mastery of Thomas Keller's The French Laundry. This upside-down caramelized apple tart is a timeless delight that captures the essence of fine dining. As you embark on this culinary journey, let the rich aroma and taste transport you to the renowned tables of The French Laundry.

Serving: Serves 8
Preparation Time: 30 minutes
Ready Time: 1 hour 30 minutes

Ingredients:
- 6 to 8 large apples, preferably a mix of Granny Smith and Golden Delicious
- 1 cup granulated sugar
- 1/2 cup unsalted butter
- 1 teaspoon vanilla extract
- 1 sheet puff pastry, thawed if frozen

Instructions:
1. Preheat the Oven:
Preheat your oven to 375°F (190°C).
2. Peel and Slice Apples:
Peel, core, and slice the apples into thick wedges. Set aside.
3. Caramelize the Sugar:
In an ovenproof skillet over medium heat, evenly sprinkle the sugar. Allow it to melt and caramelize, swirling the pan occasionally to ensure even browning. Once the caramel turns a rich amber color, add the butter and vanilla extract, stirring until well combined.
4. Arrange Apple Slices:
Remove the skillet from heat and carefully arrange the apple slices in a circular pattern over the caramel, ensuring they fit snugly. Fill any gaps with smaller pieces.
5. Cover with Puff Pastry:
Roll out the puff pastry on a floured surface to fit the skillet. Place it over the apples, tucking in the edges around the apples.
6. Bake to Perfection:

Transfer the skillet to the preheated oven and bake for 30-40 minutes or until the pastry is golden brown and crisp.

7. Invert and Serve:

Once baked, let the tart rest for a few minutes. Place a serving plate over the skillet and, using oven mitts, carefully invert the tart onto the plate. The luscious caramelized apples will now be on top.

8. Serve Warm:

Serve the Tarte Tatin warm, either on its own or with a dollop of whipped cream or a scoop of vanilla ice cream.

Nutrition Information:
(Per Serving)
- Calories: 320
- Total Fat: 18g
- Saturated Fat: 11g
- Cholesterol: 45mg
- Sodium: 110mg
- Total Carbohydrates: 40g
- Dietary Fiber: 3g
- Sugars: 25g
- Protein: 2g

Elevate your dessert experience with this Tarte Tatin inspired by the culinary brilliance of The French Laundry. Each bite is a symphony of caramelized sweetness and buttery perfection, leaving your taste buds longing for more. Enjoy the magic of French-inspired cuisine in the comfort of your own home.

81. "Pain Perdu"

Pain Perdu, meaning "lost bread" in French, is a classic dish cherished for its ability to transform stale bread into a decadent and comforting treat. This indulgent dessert, often referred to as French toast, epitomizes simplicity with its rich custard-soaked bread, crisped to perfection. Inspired by the renowned Thomas Keller's The French Laundry, this rendition promises a delightful balance of flavors and textures, perfect for any meal of the day.

Serving: 4 servings

Preparation time: 15 minutes
Ready time: 30 minutes

Ingredients:
- 8 slices of brioche or French bread, about 1/2 inch thick
- 4 large eggs
- 1 cup whole milk
- 1/4 cup granulated sugar
- 1 teaspoon vanilla extract
- 1/2 teaspoon ground cinnamon
- Pinch of salt
- Unsalted butter, for cooking
- Maple syrup, fresh berries, or powdered sugar for serving (optional)

Instructions:
1. Prepare the Custard Mixture:
- In a medium-sized mixing bowl, whisk together the eggs, milk, sugar, vanilla extract, cinnamon, and a pinch of salt until well combined. Set aside.
2. Soak the Bread:
- Dip each slice of bread into the custard mixture, ensuring both sides are thoroughly coated. Allow the bread to absorb the mixture for about 1-2 minutes per side.
3. Cook the Pain Perdu:
- Heat a non-stick skillet or griddle over medium heat and add a small amount of butter to coat the surface.
- Place the soaked bread slices onto the skillet and cook for 3-4 minutes per side, or until golden brown and slightly crispy.
4. Serve:
- Once cooked, transfer the Pain Perdu to a serving plate.
- Serve warm with maple syrup, fresh berries, or a dusting of powdered sugar, if desired.

Nutrition Information: *(per serving)*
- Calories: Approximately 320
- Total Fat: 14g
- Saturated Fat: 7g
- Trans Fat: 0g
- Cholesterol: 205mg
- Sodium: 340mg

- Total Carbohydrate: 37g
- Dietary Fiber: 1g
- Sugars: 12g
- Protein: 12g

Note: Nutrition Information is approximate and may vary based on specific ingredients used and serving sizes.

Enjoy this delightful Pain Perdu, a tribute to the timeless flavors found at Thomas Keller's iconic French Laundry restaurant.

82. "Soufflé"

Indulge your senses in the exquisite world of culinary artistry inspired by the renowned Thomas Keller's The French Laundry restaurant. Our journey begins with a delicate yet decadent creation—the Soufflé. This classic French dish, elevated to perfection at The French Laundry, promises a symphony of flavors and textures that will captivate even the most discerning palate. Prepare to embark on a culinary adventure that pays homage to the essence of fine dining.

Serving: Serves 4
Preparation Time: 15 minutes
Ready Time: 30 minutes

Ingredients:
- 4 tablespoons unsalted butter (plus extra for greasing ramekins)
- 1/4 cup all-purpose flour
- 1 cup whole milk, warmed
- 1/2 cup grated Gruyère cheese
- 1/2 cup grated Parmesan cheese
- Salt and freshly ground black pepper to taste
- Pinch of nutmeg
- 5 large egg yolks
- 6 large egg whites, at room temperature
- Pinch of cream of tartar
- 1/2 cup finely grated Comté cheese (for coating ramekins)

Instructions:
1. Preheat Oven:

Preheat the oven to 375°F (190°C). Butter and coat four 8-ounce ramekins with finely grated Comté cheese, ensuring an even coating on the bottoms and sides.

2. Prepare Roux:

In a saucepan, melt 4 tablespoons of butter over medium heat. Add the flour and whisk continuously for about 2 minutes, ensuring the mixture doesn't brown. Gradually pour in the warmed milk, whisking constantly until smooth. Cook for an additional 2-3 minutes until the mixture thickens.

3. Cheese Infusion:

Stir in the Gruyère and Parmesan cheeses until fully melted and incorporated. Season with salt, black pepper, and a pinch of nutmeg, adjusting to taste. Remove the saucepan from heat.

4. Incorporate Egg Yolks:

Quickly whisk in the egg yolks, ensuring they are well combined with the cheese mixture. Transfer the mixture to a large bowl and set aside.

5. Whip Egg Whites:

In a clean, dry bowl, whip the egg whites and cream of tartar until stiff peaks form. Gently fold one-third of the whipped egg whites into the cheese mixture to lighten it. Gradually fold in the remaining egg whites until just combined.

6. Fill Ramekins:

Divide the soufflé mixture evenly among the prepared ramekins, smoothing the tops with a spatula. Run your thumb around the inside edge of each ramekin to create a slight indentation, which encourages the soufflés to rise evenly.

7. Bake:

Place the ramekins on a baking sheet and bake in the preheated oven for 18-20 minutes or until the soufflés have risen and the tops are golden brown.

8. Serve Immediately:

Serve the soufflés immediately, as they are best enjoyed fresh out of the oven. Garnish with a sprinkle of grated Comté cheese and a touch of freshly ground black pepper if desired.

Nutrition Information:

Note: Nutritional values are approximate and may vary based on specific ingredients and portion sizes.

- Calories per serving: 320
- Total Fat: 23g

- Saturated Fat: 13g
- Trans Fat: 0g
- Cholesterol: 260mg
- Sodium: 420mg
- Total Carbohydrates: 10g
- Dietary Fiber: 0g
- Sugars: 2g
- Protein: 18g

Elevate your dining experience with this Soufflé inspired by the culinary excellence of Thomas Keller's The French Laundry. A symphony of flavors awaits, ensuring a memorable journey through the art of fine cuisine.

83. "Brioche"

Indulge in the exquisite world of French culinary mastery with this delectable Brioche recipe, inspired by the iconic menu of Thomas Keller's The French Laundry restaurant. Brioche, with its rich, buttery flavor and delicate, flaky texture, epitomizes the artistry and precision of French baking. Elevate your dining experience and bring the essence of The French Laundry into your home with this delightful treat. Perfect for breakfast, brunch, or a sweet snack, this Brioche is sure to transport you to the charming streets of Paris with every bite.

Serving: Makes 12 servings.
Preparation Time: 30 minutes.
Ready Time: 4 hours (including rising and baking time).

Ingredients:
- 1/2 cup warm whole milk (110°F/43°C)
- 2 1/4 teaspoons active dry yeast
- 1/4 cup granulated sugar, plus 1 teaspoon
- 3 1/2 cups all-purpose flour
- 1 teaspoon salt
- 4 large eggs, at room temperature
- 1 cup unsalted butter, softened
- 1 egg, beaten (for egg wash)

Instructions:

1. Activate the Yeast:
In a small bowl, combine warm milk, 1 teaspoon of sugar, and active dry yeast. Let it sit for 5-10 minutes until frothy.

2. Mix the Dough:
In a large mixing bowl, whisk together the flour, remaining sugar, and salt. Make a well in the center and add the activated yeast mixture. Stir in the eggs one at a time until well combined. Incorporate the softened butter gradually, mixing until a soft, sticky dough forms.

3. Knead the Dough:
Turn the dough onto a floured surface and knead for about 10 minutes, or until it becomes smooth and elastic. Place the dough in a lightly oiled bowl, cover it with a damp cloth, and let it rise in a warm place for 2 hours or until doubled in size.

4. Shape the Brioche:
Punch down the risen dough and divide it into two equal portions. Shape each portion into a log and place them in greased brioche molds or a loaf pan. Allow the dough to rise for an additional 1-2 hours, or until it reaches the rim of the molds.

5. Bake:
Preheat the oven to 375°F (190°C). Brush the tops of the brioche with the beaten egg for a golden finish. Bake for 25-30 minutes or until the brioche is deep golden brown. Allow it to cool in the molds for 10 minutes before transferring to a wire rack.

6. Serve:
Slice and serve the brioche warm, plain or with your favorite spreads. Pair it with a cup of coffee or tea for a truly French experience.

Nutrition Information:
Note: Nutrition information is per serving.
- Calories: 320
- Total Fat: 19g
- Saturated Fat: 11g
- Cholesterol: 120mg
- Sodium: 200mg
- Total Carbohydrates: 31g
- Dietary Fiber: 1g
- Sugars: 5g
- Protein: 7g

Indulge in the divine flavors of this French-inspired Brioche, a testament to the culinary brilliance of Thomas Keller's The French Laundry. Enjoy the delicate layers and rich, buttery taste that make this recipe a true masterpiece.

84. "Praline"

Indulge in the exquisite flavors reminiscent of Thomas Keller's iconic The French Laundry restaurant with our decadent Praline recipe. This classic confectionery, with its rich blend of caramelized nuts and sugar, captures the essence of fine dining and elevates your culinary experience. Follow these simple steps to create a dessert that mirrors the sophistication and craftsmanship of one of the world's most celebrated kitchens.

Serving: Makes approximately 20 pralines.
Preparation Time: 15 minutes
Ready Time: 1 hour

Ingredients:
- 1 cup pecan halves
- 1 cup granulated sugar
- 1/2 cup light brown sugar, packed
- 1/2 cup heavy cream
- 4 tablespoons unsalted butter
- 1 teaspoon pure vanilla extract
- 1/4 teaspoon salt

Instructions:
1. Prepare Baking Sheet: Line a baking sheet with parchment paper or a silicone baking mat. Set aside.
2. Toast Pecans: In a dry skillet over medium heat, toast the pecan halves for 3-5 minutes, stirring frequently, until fragrant. Be cautious not to burn them. Remove from heat and set aside.
3. Create Praline Mixture:
- In a heavy-bottomed saucepan, combine granulated sugar, brown sugar, and heavy cream.
- Cook over medium heat, stirring constantly until the sugar dissolves.

- Add butter and continue to stir until the mixture reaches 240°F (115°C) on a candy thermometer.

4. Incorporate Pecans and Flavorings:
- Remove the saucepan from heat and stir in the toasted pecans, vanilla extract, and salt.
- Continue stirring until the mixture thickens and the pecans are evenly coated.

5. Shape and Cool:
- Quickly drop spoonfuls of the praline mixture onto the prepared baking sheet, forming small rounds.
- Allow the pralines to cool and harden at room temperature for about an hour.

6. Serve:
- Once fully cooled, transfer the pralines to an airtight container for storage.
- Serve these delectable treats as a sweet finale to a special meal or as a delightful gift for friends and family.

Nutrition Information:
Note: Nutritional values are approximate and may vary based on specific ingredients used.
- Serving Size: 1 praline
- Calories: 120
- Total Fat: 8g
- Saturated Fat: 2g
- Trans Fat: 0g
- Cholesterol: 10mg
- Sodium: 30mg
- Total Carbohydrates: 12g
- Dietary Fiber: 1g
- Sugars: 11g
- Protein: 1g

Immerse yourself in the world of fine dining with these delectable pralines, a sweet tribute to the culinary excellence of Thomas Keller's The French Laundry.

85. "Madeleine"

Transport your taste buds to the culinary world of Thomas Keller's iconic restaurant, The French Laundry, with these delicate and irresistible Madeleines. Named after the famous French tea cake, these golden-brown treats boast a tender crumb and a subtle hint of citrus that will leave you savoring every bite. Perfect for an elegant afternoon tea or a sweet conclusion to a gourmet meal, these Madeleines capture the essence of Keller's culinary mastery.

Serving: Makes approximately 24 Madeleines
Preparation Time: 15 minutes
Ready Time: 30 minutes

Ingredients:
- 1 cup unsalted butter, melted and cooled
- 4 large eggs
- 1 cup granulated sugar
- 1 teaspoon vanilla extract
- 2 cups all-purpose flour
- 1 teaspoon baking powder
- 1/2 teaspoon salt
- Zest of 1 lemon
- Powdered sugar, for dusting (optional)

Instructions:
1. Preheat your oven to 350°F (180°C). Grease and flour Madeleine molds generously.
2. In a mixing bowl, beat the eggs and granulated sugar together until light and fluffy.
3. Add the melted butter and vanilla extract to the egg mixture, mixing well.
4. In a separate bowl, whisk together the flour, baking powder, and salt. Gradually add this dry mixture to the wet ingredients, stirring until just combined.
5. Gently fold in the lemon zest to infuse the batter with a subtle citrus flavor.
6. Spoon the batter into the prepared Madeleine molds, filling each about 2/3 full.
7. Bake for 10-12 minutes or until the edges are golden brown and the center springs back when lightly touched.

8. Remove the Madeleines from the oven and allow them to cool in the molds for a few minutes before transferring them to a wire rack to cool completely.

9. Optional: Dust the cooled Madeleines with powdered sugar for an elegant finish.

Nutrition Information:
Note: Nutritional values are approximate and may vary based on specific ingredients used.
- Calories per serving: 120
- Total Fat: 8g
- Saturated Fat: 5g
- Cholesterol: 45mg
- Sodium: 70mg
- Total Carbohydrates: 12g
- Sugars: 6g
- Protein: 2g

Indulge in the exquisite simplicity of these Madeleines, inspired by the culinary genius of Thomas Keller. Whether enjoyed with a cup of tea or as a delightful dessert, these little French delights are sure to elevate your dining experience.

86. "Coulis"

Indulge your culinary senses with the exquisite simplicity of Coulis, a versatile and vibrant sauce that elevates any dish to a new level of sophistication. Inspired by the culinary finesse of Thomas Keller's iconic The French Laundry restaurant, this Coulis recipe adds a touch of elegance to your gastronomic repertoire. Bursting with fresh flavors and a silky texture, this sauce is a testament to the artistry of fine dining.

Serving: Ideal for drizzling over desserts, accompanying savory dishes, or as a flavorful base for soups, Coulis brings a burst of color and taste to your plate. This recipe yields approximately 1 cup of Coulis.
Preparation Time: 15 minutes
Ready Time: 45 minutes

Ingredients:

- 2 cups fresh berries (such as raspberries, strawberries, or a mix)
- 1/4 cup granulated sugar
- 1 tablespoon lemon juice
- Pinch of salt

Instructions:

1. Prepare the Berries:

Rinse the fresh berries under cold water and pat them dry with a paper towel. Remove any stems or leaves, ensuring only the ripe fruit is used.

2. Cooking the Coulis:

In a medium saucepan, combine the berries, granulated sugar, lemon juice, and a pinch of salt. Cook over medium heat, stirring occasionally, until the berries start to release their juices and the sugar has dissolved. This should take approximately 10-15 minutes.

3. Simmering:

Reduce the heat to low and let the mixture simmer for an additional 20-30 minutes, allowing the berries to break down and the sauce to thicken. Stir occasionally to prevent sticking.

4. Strain the Coulis:

Once the berries have softened and the sauce has thickened, remove the saucepan from the heat. Using a fine-mesh strainer set over a bowl, strain the Coulis to remove any seeds or pulp. Use the back of a spoon to press the mixture through the strainer, extracting as much liquid as possible.

5. Cooling:

Allow the Coulis to cool to room temperature. Once cooled, refrigerate for at least 2 hours to enhance the flavors.

6. Serve and Enjoy:

Drizzle the chilled Coulis over desserts like cheesecake or panna cotta, or use it as a flavorful accompaniment to savory dishes such as grilled chicken or seafood.

Nutrition Information:

Note: Nutrition values are approximate and may vary based on the specific berries used.
- Serving Size: 2 tablespoons
- Calories: 30
- Total Fat: 0g
- Cholesterol: 0mg
- Sodium: 5mg
- Total Carbohydrates: 7g

- Dietary Fiber: 2g
- Sugars: 5g
- Protein: 0g

Elevate your dining experience with this Coulis recipe, inspired by the culinary genius of Thomas Keller's The French Laundry. It's a culinary masterpiece that transforms the ordinary into the extraordinary.

87. "Pâte à Choux"

Embark on a culinary journey inspired by the renowned Thomas Keller's The French Laundry with our exquisite recipe for Pâte à Choux. This classic French pastry dough serves as the canvas for a myriad of delightful creations, capturing the essence of the fine dining experience at The French Laundry. With its light, airy texture and versatility, Pâte à Choux is the perfect base for both sweet and savory delights, ensuring a taste of sophistication in every bite.

Serving: Makes approximately 24 small pastries
Preparation Time: 20 minutes
Ready Time: 1 hour 30 minutes

Ingredients:
- 1 cup water
- 1/2 cup unsalted butter
- 1/4 teaspoon salt
- 1 cup all-purpose flour
- 4 large eggs

Instructions:
1. Preheat your oven to 425°F (220°C). Line a baking sheet with parchment paper.
2. In a medium saucepan, combine water, butter, and salt. Bring the mixture to a boil over medium heat, stirring until the butter is melted.
3. Reduce the heat to low, add the flour all at once, and stir vigorously with a wooden spoon until the mixture forms a ball. Continue to cook for an additional 1-2 minutes, ensuring the dough doesn't stick to the pan.

4. Transfer the dough to a mixing bowl and let it cool for a couple of minutes.
5. Using an electric mixer, add the eggs one at a time, beating well after each addition. The dough should be smooth and glossy.
6. Spoon the dough into a pastry bag fitted with a plain tip (or use a Ziploc bag with the corner snipped off).
7. Pipe small mounds of dough onto the prepared baking sheet, leaving space between each.
8. Bake in the preheated oven for 10 minutes, then reduce the heat to 375°F (190°C) and bake for an additional 15-20 minutes or until golden brown and puffed.
9. Remove from the oven and let the pastries cool on a wire rack.

Nutrition Information:
(Per serving - based on 1 small pastry)
- Calories: 80
- Total Fat: 6g
- Saturated Fat: 3.5g
- Cholesterol: 55mg
- Sodium: 55mg
- Total Carbohydrates: 4g
- Dietary Fiber: 0g
- Sugars: 0g
- Protein: 2g

Elevate your culinary skills with this Pâte à Choux recipe, a tribute to the exquisite flavors and artistry found at Thomas Keller's iconic The French Laundry.

88. "Crêpe"

Indulge in the exquisite world of French cuisine with our homage to the culinary masterpiece of Thomas Keller's The French Laundry. These delicate and versatile Crêpes are a nod to the sophistication and finesse that define the iconic restaurant's menu. Perfectly thin and tender, these Crêpes serve as a canvas for both sweet and savory creations, showcasing the elegance of French culinary artistry.

Serving: Makes approximately 12 Crêpes

Preparation Time: 15 minutes
Ready Time: 30 minutes

Ingredients:
- 1 cup all-purpose flour
- 2 large eggs
- 1 1/2 cups whole milk
- 2 tablespoons unsalted butter, melted
- 1/4 teaspoon salt
- 1 tablespoon sugar (for sweet crêpes)
- Additional butter for greasing the pan

Instructions:
1. Prepare the Batter:
- In a blender, combine the flour, eggs, milk, melted butter, salt, and sugar (if making sweet crêpes). Blend until the batter is smooth and has a thin consistency. Allow the batter to rest for at least 15 minutes to ensure optimal texture.
2. Cooking the Crêpes:
- Heat a non-stick skillet or crêpe pan over medium heat. Add a small amount of butter to coat the pan.
- Pour a small amount of batter into the center of the pan, swirling it to spread the batter thinly across the surface. Cook for about 1-2 minutes or until the edges start to lightly brown.
3. Flip and Cook:
- Gently flip the crêpe using a spatula and cook the other side for an additional 1-2 minutes, or until golden. Repeat until all the batter is used, adding butter to the pan as needed.
4. Serve:
- Serve the crêpes warm, folded or rolled, with your choice of fillings. For a sweet touch, try Nutella, fresh berries, or a dusting of powdered sugar. For a savory option, consider ham and cheese, sautéed mushrooms, or spinach.

Nutrition Information:
(Per serving, based on 2 crêpes)
- Calories: 180
- Protein: 7g
- Carbohydrates: 20g
- Fat: 8g

- Saturated Fat: 4g
- Cholesterol: 70mg
- Sodium: 160mg
- Fiber: 1g
- Sugar: 4g

Elevate your dining experience with these Crêpes inspired by the timeless elegance of The French Laundry. Whether enjoyed for breakfast, brunch, or a decadent dessert, these versatile delights are sure to transport you to the heart of French culinary excellence.

89. "Fondant"

Indulge in the exquisite world of French culinary artistry with this sumptuous Fondant recipe, a delightful dessert inspired by the impeccable menu of Thomas Keller's renowned establishment, The French Laundry. Elegantly crafted and irresistibly decadent, this dessert is a testament to the mastery of flavors that defines the culinary experience at The French Laundry.

Serving: 4 servings
Preparation Time: 20 minutes
Ready Time: 25 minutes

Ingredients:
- 200g high-quality dark chocolate (70% cocoa)
- 200g unsalted butter
- 200g granulated sugar
- 4 large eggs
- 100g all-purpose flour
- 1/2 teaspoon salt
- 1 teaspoon vanilla extract
- Cocoa powder for dusting (optional)
- Whipped cream or vanilla ice cream for serving (optional)

Instructions:
1. Preheat your oven to 375°F (190°C). Grease and flour four individual ramekins or molds.

2. In a heatproof bowl, melt the dark chocolate and butter together using a double boiler or by microwaving in 30-second intervals, stirring until smooth. Allow the mixture to cool slightly.
3. In a separate bowl, whisk together the sugar and eggs until the mixture becomes pale and slightly thickened.
4. Gently fold the melted chocolate mixture into the egg and sugar mixture until well combined.
5. Sift in the flour and salt, folding gently until just combined. Be careful not to overmix.
6. Stir in the vanilla extract, ensuring an even distribution of flavors.
7. Divide the batter evenly among the prepared ramekins or molds.
8. Bake in the preheated oven for 12-15 minutes, or until the edges are set, but the center remains slightly gooey.
9. Allow the fondants to cool for a few minutes before running a knife around the edges and inverting them onto serving plates.
10. Dust with cocoa powder and serve with a dollop of whipped cream or a scoop of vanilla ice cream, if desired.

Nutrition Information:
(Per serving)
- Calories: 480
- Total Fat: 35g
- Saturated Fat: 21g
- Cholesterol: 170mg
- Sodium: 270mg
- Total Carbohydrates: 38g
- Dietary Fiber: 3g
- Sugars: 27g
- Protein: 6g

Elevate your dining experience with this divine Fondant, a perfect embodiment of the culinary excellence inspired by Thomas Keller's The French Laundry. Enjoy the harmonious blend of rich chocolate and velvety texture, leaving your taste buds in awe.

90. "Crème Brûlée"

Indulge your taste buds in the epitome of French culinary elegance with our Crème Brûlée recipe inspired by the renowned menu of Thomas

Keller's The French Laundry restaurant. This classic dessert is a symphony of creamy custard and crispy caramelized sugar, offering a luxurious experience that transcends the ordinary. Elevate your culinary skills and treat yourself to a dessert that embodies sophistication and flavor.

Serving: This recipe yields 6 servings.
Preparation Time: 15 minutes
Ready Time: 4 hours (including chilling and baking time)

Ingredients:
- 2 cups heavy cream
- 1 vanilla bean, split lengthwise, or 1 teaspoon vanilla extract
- 5 large egg yolks
- 1/2 cup granulated sugar, plus extra for caramelizing
- Pinch of salt

Instructions:
1. Preheat your oven to 325°F (163°C).
2. In a saucepan, combine the heavy cream and the vanilla bean (or vanilla extract). Heat over medium heat until it simmers, then remove from heat and let it steep for 15 minutes. If using a vanilla bean, scrape the seeds into the cream and discard the pod.
3. In a mixing bowl, whisk together the egg yolks, sugar, and a pinch of salt until the mixture becomes pale and slightly thick.
4. Slowly pour the warm cream into the egg mixture, whisking continuously to avoid curdling. Strain the custard through a fine-mesh sieve to ensure a smooth texture.
5. Divide the custard among six ramekins. Place the ramekins in a baking dish and fill the dish with hot water until it reaches halfway up the sides of the ramekins. This water bath helps ensure gentle and even baking.
6. Bake in the preheated oven for 40-45 minutes or until the custard is set around the edges but slightly jiggly in the center.
7. Remove the ramekins from the water bath and let them cool to room temperature. Once cooled, cover and refrigerate for at least 2 hours, allowing the custard to set completely.
8. Just before serving, sprinkle a thin, even layer of granulated sugar over the custard. Caramelize the sugar using a kitchen torch until it forms a golden-brown crust.

9. Allow the Crème Brûlée to sit for a few minutes to let the caramelized sugar harden, then serve and enjoy the luscious contrast of creamy custard and brittle sugar.

Nutrition Information:
(Per serving)
- Calories: 380
- Fat: 32g
- Saturated Fat: 19g
- Cholesterol: 260mg
- Sodium: 40mg
- Carbohydrates: 19g
- Sugar: 17g
- Protein: 4g

Indulge in the sublime delight of this Crème Brûlée, a masterpiece that captures the essence of The French Laundry's culinary excellence.

91. "Éclair"

Indulge in the exquisite world of French pastry with this Éclair recipe inspired by the legendary menu of Thomas Keller's iconic restaurant, The French Laundry. Éclairs are delicate, elongated pastries filled with rich pastry cream and topped with a glossy chocolate glaze. Elevate your culinary skills and treat your taste buds to the sophistication of this classic French dessert.

Serving: Makes 12 éclairs
Preparation Time: - 30 minutes
Ready Time: - 2 hours (including chilling time)

Ingredients:
For the Pastry Dough:
- 1 cup water
- 8 tablespoons unsalted butter
- 1 tablespoon granulated sugar
- 1/2 teaspoon salt
- 1 1/4 cups all-purpose flour
- 4 large eggs

For the Pastry Cream:
- 2 cups whole milk
- 1 vanilla bean, split and seeds scraped
- 6 large egg yolks
- 1/2 cup granulated sugar
- 1/3 cup cornstarch
- Pinch of salt
- 2 tablespoons unsalted butter

For the Chocolate Glaze:
- 4 ounces bittersweet chocolate, chopped
- 1/2 cup heavy cream
- 2 tablespoons unsalted butter

Instructions:

Pastry Dough:
1. In a medium saucepan, combine water, butter, sugar, and salt. Bring to a simmer over medium heat.
2. Add flour all at once and stir vigorously with a wooden spoon until the mixture forms a smooth ball.
3. Transfer the dough to a mixing bowl and let it cool for 5 minutes.
4. Add eggs one at a time, beating well after each addition, until the dough is smooth and glossy.

Piping and Baking:
5. Preheat the oven to 375°F (190°C) and line a baking sheet with parchment paper.
6. Transfer the dough to a piping bag fitted with a plain round tip. Pipe 4-inch-long strips onto the prepared baking sheet, leaving space between each éclair.
7. Bake for 25-30 minutes or until golden brown and puffed. Allow to cool completely.

Pastry Cream:
8. In a saucepan, heat the milk and vanilla bean seeds until just below boiling.
9. In a bowl, whisk together egg yolks, sugar, cornstarch, and salt until smooth.
10. Slowly pour the hot milk into the egg mixture, whisking constantly. Return the mixture to the saucepan and cook over medium heat until it thickens.
11. Remove from heat, add butter, and whisk until smooth. Let it cool, then refrigerate until chilled.

Chocolate Glaze:
12. In a heatproof bowl, combine chocolate, cream, and butter. Melt over a double boiler or in the microwave, stirring until smooth.
Assembly:
13. Cut cooled éclairs in half horizontally. Fill a piping bag with pastry cream and pipe it into the bottom halves.
14. Dip the top halves into the chocolate glaze and place them on the filled bottoms.
15. Allow the glaze to set before serving.

Nutrition Information:
(Per Éclair)
- Calories: 320
- Total Fat: 21g
- Saturated Fat: 12g
- Cholesterol: 150mg
- Sodium: 120mg
- Total Carbohydrates: 28g
- Dietary Fiber: 1g
- Sugars: 14g
- Protein: 6g

Indulge in the divine flavors of these homemade éclairs, a testament to the culinary excellence inspired by The French Laundry.

92. "Parfait"

Indulge in the exquisite elegance of a classic French dessert with our rendition of the Parfait, inspired by the culinary finesse of Thomas Keller's renowned restaurant, The French Laundry. A harmonious symphony of flavors and textures, this Parfait captivates the essence of fine dining in the comfort of your home. Layers of velvety custard, luscious fruit, and delicate crunch intertwine to create a masterpiece that pays homage to the culinary artistry of one of the world's most celebrated chefs.

Serving: 4 servings
Preparation Time: 30 minutes
Ready Time: 4 hours (including chilling time)

Ingredients:
- 1 cup heavy cream
- 1 teaspoon vanilla extract
- 1/2 cup granulated sugar
- 3 large egg yolks
- 1 cup mixed berries (strawberries, blueberries, raspberries)
- 1/2 cup granola
- 1/4 cup honey

Instructions:
1. Prepare the Custard:
a. In a medium saucepan, heat the heavy cream over medium heat until it simmers but does not boil.
b. In a separate bowl, whisk together the egg yolks and sugar until well combined.
c. Slowly pour the heated cream into the egg mixture, whisking constantly to avoid curdling.
d. Return the mixture to the saucepan and cook over low heat, stirring continuously, until it thickens enough to coat the back of a spoon.
e. Remove from heat, stir in the vanilla extract, and let it cool to room temperature.
2. Assemble the Parfait:
a. In serving glasses or bowls, layer the custard with mixed berries and granola.
b. Begin with a spoonful of custard, followed by a layer of berries, and then a sprinkle of granola. Repeat until the glass is filled, ending with a dollop of custard on top.
c. Drizzle honey over the final layer and garnish with additional berries and granola for a visually appealing presentation.
3. Chill and Serve:
a. Cover the parfait glasses with plastic wrap and refrigerate for at least 4 hours or until the custard is set.
b. Serve chilled and delight in the symphony of flavors and textures with each spoonful.

Nutrition Information:
(Per Serving)
- Calories: 380
- Total Fat: 26g

- Saturated Fat: 15g
- Cholesterol: 210mg
- Sodium: 45mg
- Total Carbohydrates: 34g
- Dietary Fiber: 3g
- Sugars: 24g
- Protein: 5g

Elevate your dessert experience with this Parfait inspired by the culinary brilliance of Thomas Keller's The French Laundry. Perfect for any occasion, it's a delightful treat that captures the essence of sophisticated dining.

93. "Gâteau"

Elevate your culinary prowess with a decadent treat inspired by the iconic menu of Thomas Keller's The French Laundry restaurant. Our "Gâteau" recipe captures the essence of French indulgence, offering a symphony of flavors and textures that will transport you to the heart of fine dining. Prepare to embark on a delightful journey as you create this exquisite dessert that pays homage to the culinary excellence of The French Laundry.

Serving: 8-10 servings
Preparation Time: 30 minutes
Ready Time: 2 hours

Ingredients:
- 1 cup all-purpose flour
- 1 cup granulated sugar
- 1/2 cup unsalted butter, softened
- 4 large eggs
- 1 teaspoon vanilla extract
- 1/2 cup whole milk
- 1 tablespoon baking powder
- 1/4 teaspoon salt
- Powdered sugar for dusting (optional)

For the Ganache:
- 8 ounces bittersweet chocolate, finely chopped

- 1 cup heavy cream
- 2 tablespoons unsalted butter

For Garnish:
- Fresh berries (strawberries, raspberries, or blueberries)

Instructions:

1. Preheat the Oven:

Preheat your oven to 350°F (175°C). Grease and flour a round cake pan.

2. Prepare the Batter:

In a large mixing bowl, cream together the softened butter and sugar until light and fluffy. Add the eggs one at a time, beating well after each addition. Stir in the vanilla extract.

3. Combine Dry Ingredients:

In a separate bowl, whisk together the flour, baking powder, and salt. Gradually add this dry mixture to the wet ingredients, alternating with the milk. Begin and end with the dry ingredients, mixing until just combined.

4. Bake:

Pour the batter into the prepared cake pan and smooth the top. Bake in the preheated oven for 25-30 minutes or until a toothpick inserted into the center comes out clean. Allow the cake to cool in the pan for 10 minutes before transferring it to a wire rack to cool completely.

5. Prepare the Ganache:

In a heatproof bowl, place the finely chopped chocolate. In a saucepan, heat the heavy cream until it just begins to boil. Pour the hot cream over the chocolate and let it sit for a minute. Add the butter and stir until smooth. Allow the ganache to cool slightly.

6. Assemble the Gâteau:

Once the cake has cooled, spread the ganache evenly over the top. Let it set for about 1 hour.

7. Garnish:

Decorate the gâteau with fresh berries just before serving. Optionally, dust with powdered sugar for an extra touch of elegance.

8. Serve and Enjoy:

Slice the gâteau into portions and serve on elegant dessert plates. Pair with a cup of coffee or a glass of dessert wine for a truly indulgent experience.

Nutrition Information:

(Per Serving)

- Calories: 350
- Total Fat: 20g
- Saturated Fat: 12g
- Cholesterol: 120mg
- Sodium: 180mg
- Total Carbohydrates: 40g
- Dietary Fiber: 2g
- Sugars: 25g
- Protein: 5g

Elevate your dessert game with this Gâteau inspired by the culinary brilliance of Thomas Keller's The French Laundry. It's a masterpiece on your plate, a celebration of flavors that will leave a lasting impression on your taste buds.

94. "Sorbet"

Indulge in the refreshing elegance of a classic sorbet, inspired by the culinary finesse of Thomas Keller's iconic restaurant, The French Laundry. This delightful frozen treat is a testament to simplicity and purity, capturing the essence of seasonal flavors in each spoonful. Perfect as a palate cleanser or a standalone dessert, this sorbet recipe embodies the culinary philosophy that has made The French Laundry a gastronomic institution.

Serving: Serves 6
Preparation Time: 15 minutes
Ready Time: 4 hours (including freezing time)

Ingredients:
- 2 cups fresh fruit puree (such as raspberry, mango, or passion fruit)
- 3/4 cup granulated sugar
- 1 cup water
- 2 tablespoons freshly squeezed lemon juice
- Zest of one lemon

Instructions:
1. Prepare the Fruit Puree:

- If using fresh fruit, wash and hull berries or peel and pit fruits as needed.
- Place the fruit in a blender or food processor and puree until smooth.
- Strain the puree to remove any seeds or pulp, ensuring a smooth texture.

2. Make the Simple Syrup:
- In a small saucepan, combine the sugar and water over medium heat.
- Stir until the sugar dissolves completely, creating a simple syrup.
- Allow the syrup to cool to room temperature.

3. Combine Ingredients:
- In a mixing bowl, combine the fresh fruit puree, simple syrup, lemon juice, and lemon zest.
- Stir until well combined, ensuring the sugar is fully dissolved.

4. Chill the Mixture:
- Refrigerate the sorbet mixture for at least 2 hours, allowing the flavors to meld.

5. Freeze:
- Transfer the chilled mixture to an ice cream maker and churn according to the manufacturer's instructions.
- Once the sorbet reaches a soft-serve consistency, transfer it to a lidded container and freeze for an additional 2 hours or until firm.

6. Serve:
- Scoop the sorbet into bowls or onto plates.
- Garnish with fresh mint or a slice of citrus for an extra touch of elegance.

Nutrition Information (per serving):
Note: Nutritional values may vary based on the chosen fruit.
- Calories: 120
- Total Fat: 0g
- Cholesterol: 0mg
- Sodium: 5mg
- Total Carbohydrates: 30g
- Dietary Fiber: 2g
- Sugars: 25g
- Protein: 1g

Elevate your dining experience with this exquisite sorbet, a nod to the culinary brilliance that defines The French Laundry's menu. Refreshing and vibrant, it's a sweet conclusion or interlude to any meal, embodying the essence of seasonal ingredients.

95. "Panna Cotta"

Indulge in the exquisite elegance of Panna Cotta, a luxurious Italian dessert that captures the essence of sophistication. This velvety creation mirrors the culinary finesse found in Thomas Keller's iconic The French Laundry restaurant. Immerse yourself in the divine simplicity of this dessert, where creamy vanilla perfection meets a delicate wobble on your palate.

Serving: Serves 6
Preparation Time: 15 minutes
Ready Time: 4 hours (including chilling time)

Ingredients:
- 2 cups heavy cream
- 1 cup whole milk
- 1/2 cup granulated sugar
- 1 vanilla bean, split lengthwise, or 1 teaspoon vanilla extract
- 2 1/4 teaspoons gelatin powder
- 3 tablespoons cold water

Instructions:
1. In a medium saucepan, combine the heavy cream, whole milk, and sugar. If using a vanilla bean, scrape the seeds into the mixture and add the pod. If using vanilla extract, reserve it for later.
2. Over medium heat, bring the mixture to a gentle simmer, stirring occasionally. Once it simmers, remove from heat and let it steep for 15-20 minutes to infuse the flavors. If using vanilla extract, add it after removing from heat.
3. In a small bowl, sprinkle gelatin over cold water. Let it sit for a few minutes until it blooms.
4. After steeping, remove the vanilla pod if used. Reheat the cream mixture until it's warm but not boiling.
5. Add the bloomed gelatin to the warm cream mixture, stirring until completely dissolved.
6. Strain the mixture through a fine-mesh sieve into a bowl to remove any undissolved gelatin or vanilla bean bits.

7. Pour the Panna Cotta mixture into ramekins or molds of your choice.
8. Refrigerate for at least 4 hours or until set.
9. Once set, run a knife around the edge of each Panna Cotta and invert onto serving plates.
10. Serve chilled, garnished with fresh berries or a drizzle of berry coulis if desired.

Nutrition Information:
(Per Serving)
Calories: 350 kcal
Protein: 4g
Fat: 32g
Carbohydrates: 15g
Sugar: 13g
Fiber: 0g
Sodium: 40mg

Delight in the divine simplicity of this Panna Cotta, a masterpiece inspired by the culinary genius of Thomas Keller's The French Laundry.

CONCLUSION

In the culinary realm, few names command as much respect and admiration as Thomas Keller, and his iconic restaurant, The French Laundry, stands as a testament to his culinary genius. "The French Laundry Feast: 95 Culinary Inspirations from Thomas Keller's Masterful Menu" takes readers on a gastronomic journey through the intricate and sophisticated world of Keller's creations. As we conclude this culinary adventure, it's evident that this cookbook is not just a collection of recipes; it's a celebration of artistry, precision, and a profound love for food.

The heart of this cookbook lies in its ability to distill the essence of The French Laundry's menu into 95 delectable food ideas. Each recipe serves as a gateway to Keller's culinary philosophy, revealing the meticulous techniques and attention to detail that define his approach. From the velvety richness of his iconic "Oysters and Pearls" to the delicate harmony of flavors in the "Butter-Poached Lobster," every dish tells a story of passion and commitment to the craft.

One cannot discuss Thomas Keller without acknowledging his dedication to the finest ingredients. The cookbook meticulously highlights the importance of sourcing top-quality produce, meats, and seafood – a hallmark of The French Laundry's commitment to excellence. Through these recipes, readers are not just given a list of instructions; they are invited to embark on a culinary pilgrimage, seeking out the best ingredients to recreate Keller's masterpieces in their own kitchens.

Beyond the technical aspects of cooking, "The French Laundry Feast" offers a glimpse into the artistry that elevates a meal into an unforgettable experience. The cookbook emphasizes the importance of presentation, guiding readers on plating techniques that transform each dish into a visual masterpiece. The carefully curated photographs accompanying the recipes serve as visual cues, inspiring home cooks to elevate their culinary skills and create plates that are not only delicious but also visually stunning.

As we explore the 95 culinary inspirations within these pages, it becomes clear that this cookbook is more than a manual for replicating The French Laundry's dishes. It is a tribute to the joy of cooking, encouraging readers to embrace the process, savor the journey, and find fulfillment in the act of creation. Each recipe is a chapter in the larger narrative of culinary exploration, inviting both seasoned chefs and aspiring home cooks to push boundaries and discover the pleasure of experimenting with flavors and techniques.

"The French Laundry Feast" is not just a cookbook; it's an invitation to celebrate the art of dining. It beckons readers to gather friends and family around the table, creating moments of joy and connection through the shared experience of exquisite food. It encapsulates the essence of Thomas Keller's culinary legacy, inspiring a new generation of cooks to approach the kitchen with curiosity, passion, and a commitment to excellence.

In conclusion, "The French Laundry Feast" is a culinary masterpiece that extends beyond the confines of its pages. It is a celebration of Thomas Keller's influence on the gastronomic world, offering a glimpse into the soul of The French Laundry's kitchen. As readers embark on their culinary adventures armed with these 95 inspirations, they carry with them not just recipes but a profound appreciation for the beauty and artistry of cooking.

Printed in Great Britain
by Amazon